the painter's handbook

A QED BOOK

Published in the United States by
GALLERY BOOKS
An imprint of W.H. Smith Publishers Inc.
112, Madison Avenue
New York, New York 10016

ISBN 0-8317-0470-5

First published in the United States in 1984

This book was designed and produced by
QED Publishing Limited, 32, Kingly Court, London W1

Printed in Hong Kong by Leefung Asco
Printers Limited

the painter's handbook

Series Consultant Editors:
Stan Smith and
Professor H.F. Ten Holt

GALLERY BOOKS
An Imprint of W. H. Smith Publishers Inc.
112 Madison Avenue
New York City 10016

Contents

Principles of painting and drawing.

History. Shape and form. Proportion. **Perspective:** Principles, History. **Color:** Theories and principles.

Principles of drawing History

Art rules and principles have been formulated after much experiment and of course they must be known before they can be broken or ignored to satisfy personal aesthetic values. The subject and the artist's intuition and feel—not the rules—should always be the guiding force.

Shape and form

European Renaissance artists were deeply concerned with rules of proportion, but the shape of the space between objects in a picture is as important as the solidity of those objects. Shape is a part of form and a work of art may be seen as consisting of form and content.

The forms of an art work are its individual masses, shapes or groupings, and how the artist presents the subject matter. Form is the result of the artist's creative intent, organization, design and composition and how he or she handles the materials.

Proportion

It is usually necessary to have good perspective and consequently good proportions to create realistic illusions. In this context 'realistic' means giving an impression of solidity or three-dimensionality. In any composition, proportion is the mathematical relationship of the parts to the whole and to each other. The 'Golden Mean', for example, was a general law of proportion first in architecture and then applied to painting and sculpture.

The 'Golden Mean' was first worked out in the first century BC by Vitruvius in his treatise *De Architectura* to establish standards for the proportions of columns, rooms and buildings. It was based on the concept of the ratio between two unequal parts of a whole, where the proportion of the smaller to the larger is equal to that of the larger to the whole.

In figure drawing, the 'Golden Mean' provided for a continuous halving of the body lengths and of the sections of the lengths resulting from each previous division. It dictated, for example, that the distance from the foot to the knee was half the length of the whole leg and that the whole leg was half that of the whole body.

The 'Golden Mean' was also used to determine the ideal proportions of a rectangle, where the longer side is equal in length to the diagonal of a square the side of which is equal to the shorter side of the rectangle: a 5 to 8 ratio or, more accurately, 0.618 to 1. The width is five-eights of the length.

During the Renaissance, the 'Golden Mean' was referred to as the 'Divine Proportion' in a work of that title published in 1509 and illustrated by Leonardo da Vinci (1452–1519). Albrecht Dürer (1471–1528) wrote a treatise on the application of proportion to figure drawing.

Some art historians believe that Egyptian and Greek art and architecture of the fifth century BC used a concept of proportion which they term dynamic symmetry because it related closely to the symmetry of living things—such as the ratio of leaves to the plants that produce them.

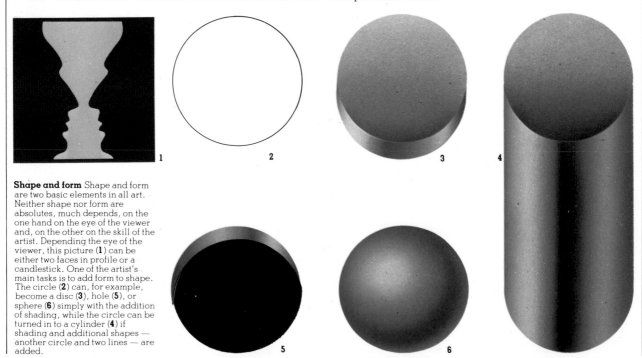

Shape and form Shape and form are two basic elements in all art. Neither shape nor form are absolutes, much depends, on the one hand on the eye of the viewer and, on the other on the skill of the artist. Depending the eye of the viewer, this picture (**1**) can be either two faces in profile or a candlestick. One of the artist's main tasks is to add form to shape. The circle (**2**) can, for example, become a disc (**3**), hole (**5**), or sphere (**6**) simply with the addition of shading, while the circle can be turned in to a cylinder (**4**) if shading and additional shapes — another circle and two lines — are added.

The Golden Section This principle, important particularly in the Renaissance, governed the ideal proportions of a rectangle where the sides are in the proportion of 5:8. These proportions were seen in nature.

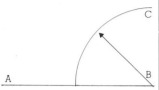

1. Divide the line A-B into two sections of equal length.

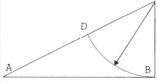

2. Put the point of the compass on B and draw an arc from the midpoint of the line to point C, at right angles to A-B.

3. Join C to points A and B. This forms a right-angled triangle.

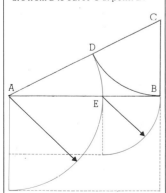

4. With the compass on C, draw an arc from B to cut A-C at point D.

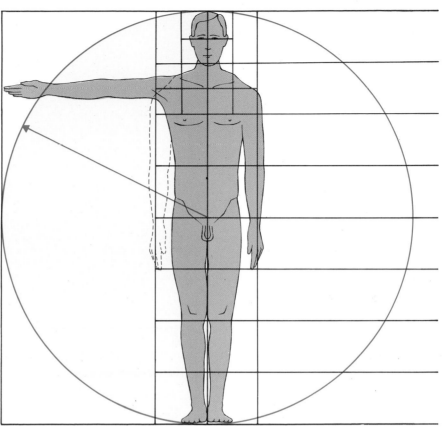

5. With the compass on A, draw an arc from B to cut A-B at point E. In proportion, E-B is to A-E as A-E is to A-B. A rectangle can be now drawn according to the golden section.

Proportion The rules and laws governing proportion have occupied artists since earliest times. During the Renaissance, artists such as Leonardo da Vinci and Albrecht Dürer began to apply the principles of proportion to the study of the human body. This development, which was accompanied by the first scientific explorations of human anatomy, perhaps reflects that age's preoccupation with Man. It was found that the body divides into eight equal sections and that these divisions almost exactly reflect the proportions of the Golden Mean. For example, the head, if measured from the chin to the crown, is one eighth of the height of the whole body, and the navel is at five eighths of the height of the whole body from the ground. This way of dividing the body in proportion is an extremely useful guide for all artists, whether beginner or expert.

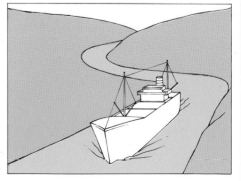

Scale In painting, scale is particularly important. The scale in a painting or drawing can be determined by the shapes in the foreground. For example, in the two pictures (**above**) the same background is given an entirely different scale according to whether the image in the foreground is the ship or a bird.

Perspective Development and Principles

P erspective is a system of creating an illusion of three dimensions in objects drawn on a two-dimensional surface. Although an important technique, it should not be allowed to become more important than the subject.

Principles

The artist's eye, or the position from which the object is seen and drawn, is called the station point or point of sight. A line representing the position of the horizon is the horizon line or eye level.

The horizontal plane where the artist stands is the ground plane. Perspective is formed on the picture plane (also known as the perspective plane or plane of delineation). This is perpendicular to the point of sight, and where it meets the horizontal plane it forms what is termed the ground line.

The center of vision or principal point is that point on the horizon line immediately opposite the position of the eye, established by the intersection of a straight line drawn at right angles from the station point to the picture plane.

Vanishing points are where parallel lines appear to converge at one or more points. A measuring point is a point on a vanishing line from which lines are projected to the picture plane so that perspective heights and widths can be measured.

Perspective can be separated into aerial and linear categories. Aerial perspective is related to atmospheric effects on objects in space—as can be seen, for instance, in the changing tones of receding hills with distance being conveyed by diminishing the intensity of the color.

The layman's idea of perspective is usually that of the plane-linear perspective seen in architectural drawings where objects closer to the point of sight appear bigger than those further away.

Various aspects of linear perspective can be considered by envisaging a cube. If one of its faces is parallel to the picture plane, all parallel lines seem to converge to a single vanishing point and the picture conveys what is known as parallel or one-point perspective.

In two-point or angular perspective, a cube is placed so that two of its faces are oblique to the picture plane and parallel lines appear to converge on two vanishing points on the horizon. With three-point or oblique perspective, three of the cube's defining faces are turned obliquely to the picture plane and parallel lines seem to converge on two points on the horizon line with another point either below or above that line. There can be as many extra vanishing points— accidental points—as there are extra systems of parallel lines. A terrestrial accidental point is below the horizon, an aerial one above.

Curvilinear perspective, as its name suggests, is made on a curved rather than a flat picture plane. Cylindrical or panorama perspective shows the picture like a panorama and the picture plane may be a cylinder. Spherical perspective is projected on a

Perspective In one point perspective, only two faces of the cube are visible and receding lines appear to meet at the vanishing point. In two point perspective, three planes of the cube are visible and two sets of lines can be drawn to converge at the vanishing points. If the cube is well above or below the viewer's horizon, three sets of lines appear to converge. Three point perspective thus includes vertical as well as horizontal lines.

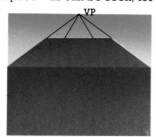

One point perspective

VP = Vanishing point

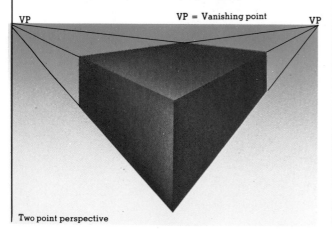

Two point perspective

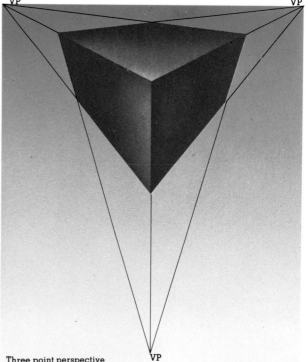

Three point perspective

spherical picture plane. A good example of this is when a photograph is taken with a wide-angle lens and lines which are usually straight appear bowed. Images in a convex mirror show this, as in *Giovanni Arnolfini and his Wife* by Jan van Eyck (*c.* 1390–1441) and the *Self Portrait* by Francesco Parmigianino (1503–1540).

History

The ancient Egyptians attempted to convey foreshortening by overlapping objects and suggested distance by drawing objects bigger, smaller, higher, lower or in strata. The Greeks understood some fundamental principles of perspective in the sixth century BC, and were familiar with foreshortening. By the next century they were using aerial perspective, implying a horizontal plane by representing shadows of objects. The Romans also used aerial or atmospheric perspective with changing colors and shades conveying the illusion of distance and depth.

However, it was not until the Renaissance that perspective became codified into a system similar to that followed by Western artists today. Pioneers of this included the architects Brunelleschi (1377–1446) and Alberti (1404–1472) and the painter Paolo Uccello (1396–1475). Leonardo da Vinci saw perspective space in a formal linear framework. His study for the *Adoration of the Kings* (*c.*1481) showed a knowledge of one-point perspective.

The search for the rules of perspective was long and varied. Alberti's concept of perspective was correct but technically difficult to apply. It involved measuring distances with a plan of squares with connecting diagonals—the tiers-points. Albrecht Dürer in 1525 used a network of squares known as craticulation, while Vignola simplified the practical construction of the perspective drawing in 1583. In 1630 De Vries used Dürer's theory and devised rules for finding vanishing points.

Such studies had an impact in painting. Uccello's *Vase* was drawn according to a system of proportions and vanishing points laid down by Brunelleschi and Alberti. Michelangelo da Caravaggio in *Supper at Emmaus*, dramatic with its sweeping contours and color, employs many vanishing points. However, painters from as early as Piero della Francesca (*c.*1415–1492) and Vermeer (1632–1675) to Canaletto (1697–1768) knew that it was not possible to transfer all that the eye could see on to a flat surface without some distortion—as is obvious in drawing a two dimensional 'map' of the world. So they tended to avoid putting geometrical patterns, in which distortions would stand out, in the outer edges of their pictures.

Things have changed, however. Modern painters often deliberately distort perspective to alter shapes and space; or, as with the modern Dutch artist Piet Mondrian (1872–1944), use blocks of color and geometric patterns to express certain feelings and ideas. Some go even further and deny any system of rules whatever.

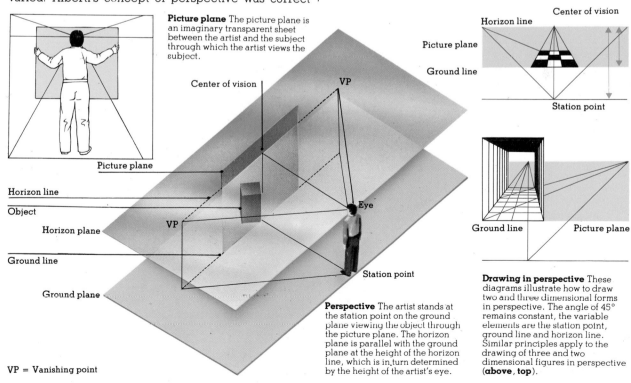

Picture plane The picture plane is an imaginary transparent sheet between the artist and the subject through which the artist views the subject.

Center of vision

Picture plane

Horizon line

Object

Horizon plane

Ground line

Ground plane

VP

VP = Vanishing point

VP

Center of vision

Eye

Station point

Perspective The artist stands at the station point on the ground plane viewing the object through the picture plane. The horizon plane is parallel with the ground plane at the height of the horizon line, which is in turn determined by the height of the artist's eye.

Center of vision

Horizon line

Picture plane

Ground line

Station point

Ground line

Picture plane

Drawing in perspective These diagrams illustrate how to draw two and three dimensional forms in perspective. The angle of 45° remains constant, the variable elements are the station point, ground line and horizon line. Similar principles apply to the drawing of three and two dimensional figures in perspective (**above**, **top**).

Color Theories and Principles

Purely scientific principles involving direct and reflected light of different colors—and thus different wavelengths—are more the concern of the physicist than the practising artist; but this has not prevented artists from trying to evolve 'scientific' theories of color harmony, or scientists attempting to apply theoretical discipline to the artist's subjective perception of color.

All painters use color and color quality to achieve the effects they seek. Even the Romans, for example, used color to indicate perspective while Renaissance painters—particularly the Venetian school—used warm and cool tones in juxtaposition to emphasize form and shape.

The earliest attempt to formulate a set of principles based on applied science was made by Michel-Eugène Chevreul in Paris. He was chief of the dyeing department at the Gobelin tapestry workshop. His treatise published in 1838 was translated into English in 1872 as *The Principles of Harmony and Contrast of Colors*. He described harmonies of similar colors and harmonies of contrasts; and devised tables of induced color effects.

The critic and art historian Charles Blanc followed Chevreul in 1867 with *Grammaire des Arts du Dessin*. The American Ogden Rood in *Modern Chromatics* (1879) arranged color combinations in pairs and triads to discover principles of harmony. David Sutter in *Les Phénomènes de la Vision* (1880) believed it was possible to learn laws of aesthetic harmony as one learned music harmony.

Delacroix (1798–1863) and the Impressionists were greatly influenced by Chevreul, developing and improving his ideas over a long period. For example, Seurat (1859–1891) applied Chevreul's principles in his paintings *Une Baignade* and *La Grande Jatte*. He covered his canvasses with tiny dots of color—the pointilliste technique—chosen and arranged to merge at viewing distance into the harmonies suggested by Chevreul.

In the twentieth century color theories have been less influential. A group of revolutionary Post-Impressionist painters which included Henri Matisse (1869–1954), André Derain (1880–1954), Maurice de Vlaminck (1876–1958), Raoul Dufy (1877–1953) and Georges Rouault (1871–1958) broke away from the earlier masters and rejected certain principles including the breaking-up of color. A critic described them as *les Fauves*—the wild beasts—because of the wild lawlessness with which they used color and sometimes form. 'Fauve' technique was to express in brilliant, explosive colors what the artists believed to be the inner qualities of the subject rather than its actual appearance. They responded emotionally to color,

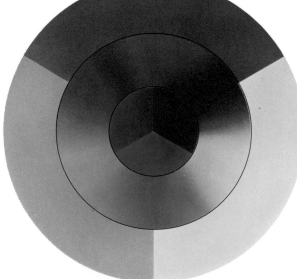

Mixing colors Combining colors (**left**) to create new colors or a variety of shades is an important element in painting. The Primary colors in painting are red, blue and yellow (**left**). Combining red and yellow produces orange; a mixture of blue and yellow makes green. Mixing red and blue does not create a clearly defined color, it makes a brownish purple.
Color wheel A color wheel (**above**) indicates the colors produced by combining the different primaries.

using it without the theory-oriented restrictions which had influenced earlier artists.

Many artists, although making use of techniques based on theory, have had harsh words for theories as such. Renoir (1841–1919) commented that nature destroyed theories. Cézanne (1839–1906), Kandinsky (1866–1944) and Matisse felt that theories were difficult to make—and even more difficult to hold up.

Piet Mondrian (1872–1944), co-founder in 1917 of the architectural style called *De Stijl*, wanted to create a purely logical art. He excluded all secondary colors and diagonals and curves, drawing only rectangular colored areas in primary colors or black and white bounded by heavy black lines.

Optical illusion art, or op art as it came to be called in the 1960s, is a style in which sharp-edged, abstract patterns produce a 'dazzle' illusion of movement. If color rather than black and white is used and certain complementary colors are placed beside each other, the dazzle effect is increased. Op art has been successfully adapted to textile designs.

With all the color theories, principles and analyses, no precise and universal concept has evolved—and possibly cannot evolve. For each artist sees color in a subjective and therefore possibly different way from another. Harmonies are evolved by artists from experiment and personal aesthetics.

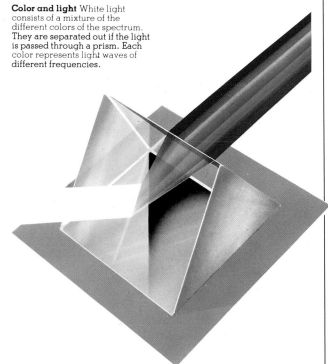

Color and light White light consists of a mixture of the different colors of the spectrum. They are separated out if the light is passed through a prism. Each color represents light waves of different frequencies.

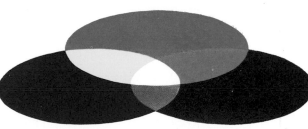

Additive primaries Red, green and blue are classified as additive primary colors because, when they are combined, white light is produced. It is extremely important for any artist to be aware of the color properties of light. When any two of the additive primaries are combined, a third color is formed. This is known as the complementary of the third color — thus yellow is the complementary of blue.

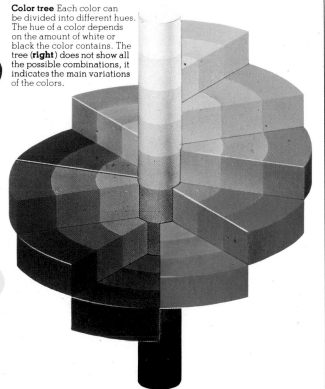

Color tree Each color can be divided into different hues. The hue of a color depends on the amount of white or black the color contains. The tree (**right**) does not show all the possible combinations, it indicates the main variations of the colors.

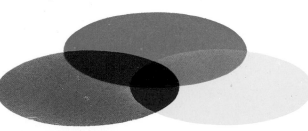

Subtractive primaries The colors formed when two of the additive primaries are combined are known as subtractive primaries. The colors thus produced are cyan (a mixture of blue and green with no red), yellow (a mixture of red and green without blue), and magenta (red and blue, with no green). If white light is passed through filters of all three subtractive primaries, black is produced.

Color hues and values A color computer (below) is a useful aid to the artist in identifying colors and establishing complementary color harmonies. Color harmony can be established using either closely associated hues of the same color, or using complementary colors. The rotating color wheel helps the artist to visualize the color harmonies. The computer cannot give the full range, but it provides a good working guide. The other side of the color computer illustrates different color mixtures.

Perception of color The individual's perception of color is affected by the background color (**right**).

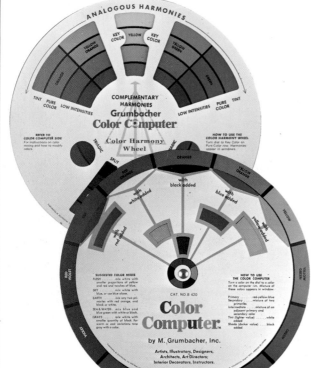

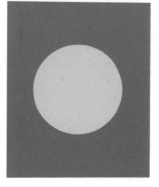

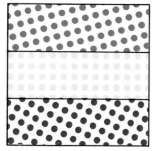

Process colors 1. In printing, a full color reproduction is created using small dots of cyan, yellow and magenta.

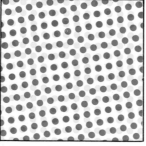

2. Cyan and yellow combine to produce green.

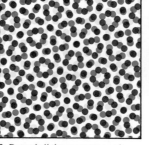

3. Dots of all three process colors are seen here in combination.

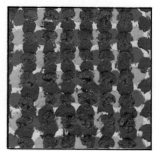

Pointillism In painting, pointillist technique uses dots to create apparently solid colors and subtle tonal variations.

Oils.

History. Constituents and properties: Binders, Diluents, Varnishes, Mediums, Dryers. **Supports:** Fabric, Wood or paper, Metal. **Preparing the canvas:** Size, Grounds. **Equipment:** Paints, Brushes, Knives, Palettes, Dippers, Mahl sticks, Easels. **Techniques.**

Oil painting History

The Flemish painter Jan van Eyck (c.1390–1441) has been called the inventor of oil painting; and although historians may argue about the technical accuracy of this description—since oil had been used as a medium for pigment many years before—his discoveries and techniques certainly laid the foundations for the art.

Around 1420, when he found that one of his egg tempera paintings had split in the sun, van Eyck experimented to find an oil that would dry in the shade. He hit on a formula consisting of a little Bruges white varnish, a kind of turpentine, mixed with linseed or nut oil. He first used this as a varnish for the tempera, in which pigments were mixed with yolk of egg; then started mixing his raw pigments directly with the oil mixture.

Not only did this dry satisfactorily out of the sun, but he discovered he could apply his colors in transparent layers or glazes, giving an inner luminosity to his paintings. He found, too, that he could correct shades and colors without spoiling their original brightness.

A follower of van Eyck, Antonello da Messina (1430–1479) spread the use of oil paint to Venice, where Giovanni Bellini (1430–1516) succeeded in achieving something like van Eyck's beauty of surface and glowing color. But it was a pupil of Bellini, Titian (1490–1576), who started to develop the full potentialities of the 'new' oil technique.

He laid in the picture lightly in monochrome, then painted the lighter parts with thicker, opaque color. Shadows were painted thinly and glazes of transparent color gave a glowing depth to the whole. The brilliance, fluidity of design and depth of tone were the hallmarks of this 'classical' technique.

The next marked advance in oil painting came with Rubens (1577–1640). He worked from a white ground with a thin gray wash, laying down his tonal and linear design in a golden umber on top of which he used cool, semi-opaque half-tones showing some of the underpainting. The dark shadows on one side of the half-tones and the brighter, lighter tones on the other side were thin coats, finished in part with transparent glaze.

Rubens influenced both Velasquez (1599–1660) and Rembrandt (1606–1669), although both masters added their own variations. Velasquez painted tastefully and sensitively, with supple but sometimes thick brushwork.

His portrait, *Lady With a Fan*, shows this rather haunting sensitivity. Rembrandt often worked areas of his paintings in a single solid color which was later covered with glazes and opaque strokes of brushwork. His method of grisaille—covering white or gray modelling with light glazes of color—became an accepted technique by the eighteenth century and was used by Reynolds (1723–1792) among others.

Such a laborious glaze-layering technique, except in the hands of a master, was thought by some artists to lead to heaviness and a lack of spontaneity. Two artists who reacted against it and returned to the freer, more direct style of Rubens—if not to his precise methods—were the English artist Gainsborough (1727–1788) and the Spanish master Goya (1746–1828).

In the eighteenth century, professional colormen were already putting ready-made oil colors in skin bladders—forerunners of the metal tubes of the mid-nineteenth century. This was a boon to out-of-the-studio artists and pioneering landscape painters such as Constable (1776–1837), but some artists and art historians regretted the move away from total control of the medium which they believed could only be achieved by craftsmen-painters who made, or supervised the making of, paints in their own studios.

However, the increasing range, flexibility and availability of prepared colors signalled the establishment of new, more direct techniques and new standards of craftsmanship. As an exponent of direct vision in the open air and with his analysis of 'broken' light, William Turner (1775–1851) became the direct precursor of the Impressionists.

The chief characteristic of the Impressionists, including Monet (1840–1926), Cézanne (1839–1906), Pissarro (1831–1903) and Sisley (1839–1899), was their broken-color technique in which strokes or dabs of opaque color were laid side by side to blend into the correct tones in the eye of the viewer. As they tried to 'paint light', their palettes contained few earth-colors and no black.

Quite early in the twentieth century, consideration of the Impressionists, and the highly individual, tradition-scorning techniques of van Gogh (1853–1890) and Gauguin (1848–1903), led many artists to the conclusion that there was no single 'right' way to paint at all.

However, before an oil painter can develop a personal technique, it is still necessary for him or her to learn something about the limitations as well as the potentialities of the medium.

The contrast in approach has perhaps never been greater. On the one hand, artists such as Salvador Dali (born 1904) use a technique of building up layers of paint which is in a direct line of descent from van Eyck. On the other hand, artists such as the Abstract Expressionists particularly Jackson Pollock (1912–1956) have extended the scope of oil painting to include previously unheard of approaches, such as throwing paint onto the canvas and allowing it to drip. Oil painting still demands a high degree of skill and knowledge. If the paint is not of a suitable consistency or is applied in a careless manner, the painting will deteriorate. This applies today as much as it did in the time of Leonardo, whose paintings have often suffered because of his excessive use of oil in his paints. Technique is closely linked to the materials being used.

Oil paints Constituents and Properties

Basically, oil paint for artists consists of dyes or pigments mixed with binders such as linseed and poppy oils which oxidize in the air and form solid skins in which the particles of color are evenly distributed.

The chemistry of the oxidation process causes gases to form under the drying oil. These force their way through the surface layer, making it porous and admitting more oxygen to the layer beneath so that the process is continuous until a solid skin is formed.

If paint is applied in layers, the first coat must be dry before the next is laid on. The second or subsequent layer usually contains more oil than the first. This is absorbed by the pores in the lower layer. The process is known as the 'fat over lean' principle. The paint surface can be varied—opaque or transparent, matt or gloss—according to the amounts of oil and thinners used by the artist.

Binders

Linseed oil is the most widely-used of all binders. It comes in various forms and qualities.

Raw linseed oil is obtained by steam-heating the flax before pressing the seeds. This produces a good quantity of oil, but it is dark and of poor quality for most painting purposes.

The finest quality oil is made by cold-pressing the flax seeds, but it is expensive and not easy to obtain. The best substitute is refined linseed oil, produced by bleaching and purifying steam-pressed oil with sulphuric acid and water. The sulphuric acid and water are then removed. The resulting oil varies from pale straw to golden amber or deep gold. It is better to use an oil from the middle of that range rather than a light one which may turn dark with age.

Stand oil, as thick and viscous as honey, is produced by treating linseed oil under heat and in a vacuum to change its molecular structure. It dries to a smooth, enamel-like film which is free of brush marks and does not become as dark with age as other linseed oils. It can be thinned with turpentine, making it a good ingredient into which to grind pigment for glazes.

Linseed oil was once sun-refined—oxidized, bleached and thickened—by standing it in the sun for several weeks in glass jars. This was the version of stand oil used by Rubens.

Poppy oil, expressed from the seed of the opium poppy, is very light in color when fresh and is used as a medium for whites and pale colors, keeping them bright and clear. But it is a slow dryer and cracks more easily than linseed with age. It is useful for *alla prima* painting or in modifying a linseed oil color.

Walnut oil, obtained by cold-pressing young walnuts, is pale, thin, and a faster dryer than poppy—almost as fast as linseed. However, it is costly, not easily obtainable and cannot be kept for long periods without going rancid.

There are many other naturally-drying vegetable oils which can be used by painters, including safflower, tung, oiticica and stillingia, but none have the versatility of linseed and poppy oils.

Artificial drying oils can be made by adding chemicals such as manganese or cobalt to vegetable oils. They can cause cracks and discoloring if not correctly mixed and used, but they are useful in damp conditions; and ready-prepared mixtures are available from some colormen.

Diluents

Solvents and thinners, which are called diluents, are added to paints ground in oils or varnishes to give them the right consistency for application. Those in current use include turpentine, oil of spike, refined petroleum, gasoline, benzol and acetone.

An ideal thinner should evaporate evenly and completely and mix thoroughly with all the other ingredients in the medium in any ratio without reacting chemically with them. It should not dissolve the underpainting, its fumes should not be harmful to the user, its odor should soon disappear from the dried film, and it should not be readily inflammable.

While research chemists work on the problem—and there have been recent advances in the field—the nearest to this ideal is the familiar turpentine, distilled from the gum of pine trees.

There is a wide range of quality. That sold for art purposes is known as rectified turpentine, doubly distilled and purified, and should not leave a ring or stain when blobbed on to blotting paper. A passable quality of turpentine can be bought in quantity from paint stores where it goes under the name of pure gum spirits of turpentine.

Two other turpentines, which still contain their natural gum or resin, are occasionally used by artists. They are Venice turpentine, from the exudation of larch trees; and Strasbourg turpentine, from the Tyrolean silver fir.

Mineral or white spirits, distilled from crude petroleum oils, is similar in its properties to turpentine and has replaced it in industrial paints. But although it leaves no sticky residue and does not deteriorate with age, many artists do not like using it in the studio. It has an unpleasant benzine-like smell and, since damar resin is not fully soluble in it, cannot be used in making damar varnish medium.

Gasoline or petrol was once quite widely used as a thinner, but lost popularity with the addition of substances which made it more valuable as an automobile fuel—and useless in the studio.

Varnishes

Varnishes, which are basically resins in solvents, have been used in oil painting for many centuries. They have been used as pigment-binding media for glazes, and for paint protection.

They are divided into hard and soft varnishes: hard

when the resin is dissolved in an oil such as linseed; soft when turpentine is the solvent.

Simple solution varnishes which can be made in the studio have many uses. Picture varnish can be used to provide a final protective coat for the painting. Retouch varnish contains more turpentine so that it does not leave a high-gloss skin. Mixing varnish is used for adding to tube colors to make glazes. Isolating varnish, for use over recently-dried oil paint, acts as sizing between the coats and allows overpainting and correction without affecting the underpaint.

Damar varnish, which is damar resin dissolved in turpentine, stays colorless longer than other common varnishes because of its lack of impurities. It can be bought ready-made. To make it in the studio, break the resin into small pieces, wrap in muslin or cheesecloth and suspend the bag in a container of turpentine. Make sure the wrapped resin does not touch the side of the container, which should be covered to keep out dust. The solution should be ready for use in two or three days.

To make damar varnish medium for glazing, mix nine parts of the varnish with nine parts of turpentine, four parts of stand oil and two parts of Venice turpentine. If it is to be used for overpainting, an extra drop or two of stand oil in the mixture ensures an oilier, more flexible surface. A simple thick varnish medium for glossy glazes can be made by adding one part of stand oil to three parts of Venice turpentine.

Mastic resin, dissolved in turpentine, is easier to use than damar varnish, but tends to yellow in time. The bad preservation of many eighteenth and nineteenth century paintings is often put down to the use of megilp, a thick medium made from mastic varnish and linseed oil.

Mastic and sandarac were the main resins used in early painting. Sandarac, from a North African tree, is very hard, and a simple solution can only be made in strong solvents such as alcohol; but it can be 'cooked' into a varnish by dissolving it in heated oil. The surface it gives is liable to be very brittle.

Shellac makes a strong, hard but flexible varnish. Its main use in painting is as a sizing for a ground which is too porous. It can be made in the studio by slowly adding broken white or brown shellac to alcohol—in the proportion of one part of the resin to seven parts of the solvent—and shaking the mixture until all the shellac is dissolved.

Synthetic gels for mixing with tube paints are now on

Raw linseed oil

Stand linseed oil

Drying linseed oil

Cold pressed linseed oil

Refined linseed oil

sale. Synthetic resins form the base of most of our household enamels, paints and varnishes, replacing materials of natural origin. Laboratory resins include polyester, vinyl, epoxy, plastics and—most interesting to the artist—alkyd and acrylic resins.

Alkyd paints have now been made up into an artists' range by Winsor and Newton. They can be thinned with turpentine or white spirits and used with oil media. Their main advantages are that they dry within 18 hours and resist cracking and yellowing. If quick drying is not desired for some reason, the process can be slowed down by adding petroleum distillate.

Mediums

Wax added to oil varnishes produces a matt surface. This is vulnerable, however. Rubbing it makes it smooth and shiny, as with a wax polish. Artists may like to experiment with varying proportions of wax to produce different effects.

Beeswax medium is made by warming one part of fragmented white beeswax to three parts of turpentine in a double boiler. Stir until dissolved and, when cool, store in a wide-necked container.

Beeswax oil medium is thick, dark and discolors pigments mixed with it; but its versatility—it was used by Rubens—can compensate for this disadvantage. It is a drying medium and can be stirred into thick paint for impasto and into thin paint for glazing. The drying element in it is litharge, a form of lead monoxide. This heavy yellow powder is poisonous and must be used with care. Take ten parts of raw linseed oil, two parts

of beeswax and one-sixteenth part of litharge. Mix the litharge first with a little oil. Slowly warm the rest of the oil in a large metal container. The next part of the process should be carried out near an extractor fan or even in the open, avoiding the fumes. Add the litharge and small pieces of beeswax to the warm oil, stir and heat to 250°C, or until the mixtures looks black and gives off brown fumes. When the mixtures cools, pour into wide-necked containers and cover. The liquid sets like wax.

Maroger's medium, which has been popular for years and is pleasant to use, can be bought ready-made. It consists of an emulsion of boiled linseed oil, mastic varnish, gum arabic and water. Two nineteenth century media still available are Bell's: brown linseed oil thinned with spike oil; and Robertson's: copal varnish, poppy oil and white wax.

Dryers

Dryers, which are also called siccatives, are metallic salts mixed with the normal paint and varnish ingredients. They may affect permanence adversely, but have as old a history as drying oils themselves. Some pigments are naturally fast dryers and only very small amounts of the drying ingredients—lead, cobalt or manganese—are needed. The thin glazes of many of the early Masters contain them. Pictures in which drying media have been used throughout should be given a thin coat of protective varnish immediately they are thoroughly dry. A normal painting can take several months to dry before it is ready for varnishing.

Sun bleached poppy oil

Sun bleached linseed oil

Drying poppy oil

Purified linseed oil

Walnut oil

Drying oils for oil painting
Linseed oil is the most versatile and widely used binder for oil paint. It is available in various forms for use as a binder or medium. The flow, texture and drying rate of oil paint depend on the type of oil used. Stand linseed oil retards the drying speed, but improves the flow of the paint whereas drying linseed oil speeds up the drying process. Cold pressed and refined oils give greater transparency to the paint but are relatively slow-drying. Sun bleached linseed and poppy oils are both mediums which improve the flow of the paint but linseed is the more quick drying. The advantage of poppy oil is that it is light in color and keeps pale colors fresh and clear. Walnut oil is less commonly used than linseed oil, although it dries almost as fast; it is more expensive and difficult to find, and does not keep well.

Ingredients for varnishes and varnish mediums Resinous varnishes can be used as a protective layer over finished work and may also be mixed with solvents such as turpentine and alcohol and with oils and wax, to make a wide range of mediums to be mixed with the paint. These vary the transparency or plasticity of the paint and also affect the drying speed of the paint and the flexibility of the finished surface. Many preparations are now commercially available ready-made, but it is possible, and often desirable, to make up the varnishes as required from basic ingredients. The following substances are used in the preparation of various basic varnishes and varnish mediums: (from **left** to **right**) copal varnish, linseed oil, turpentine, damar varnish, stand oil, Venice turpentine, shellac, alcohol, damar resin, beeswax, litharge. White spirit cannot be substituted for turpentine in making up a varnish, as it is harsh and may devalue the color of the paint as it dries. It is not possible use it with damar resin, which will not dissolve in white spirit.

Varnish medium
1 part copal varnish
1 part linseed oil
1 part turpentine
Pour the measured ingredients into a clean, dry bottle and shake well until the liquids are blended. This makes a basic, thick varnish medium which dries quickly and can be further thinned if required.

Damar varnish
1 part crushed damar resin
4 parts turpentine
Put the turpentine in a pot. Wrap the resin in muslin and tie it so that it is suspended in the pot of turpentine but does not touch the sides of the container. Cover the pot so that no dust falls into it, and leave it to stand for two or three days. The resin gradually dissolves and a varnish is produced which will not yellow with age. The process can be speeded up slightly by occasional agitation of the muslin bag.

Damar varnish medium
9 parts damar varnish
9 parts turpentine
4 parts stand oil
2 parts Venice turpentine
Pour all the ingredients into a clean, dry bottle and shake it vigorously until the substances are completely mixed. This medium can be encouraged to dry more quickly by adding one drop of cobalt drier for each pint of liquid. Damar varnish medium is clear and is used to thin paint for glazing.

Stand oil medium
1 part stand oil
3 parts Venice turpentine
Pour the liquids into a jar or bottle and shake well until they are blended together. This medium retains the gloss and brilliance of the paint as it dries.

Shellac varnish
1 part shellac (white or brown)
7 parts alcohol
Put the alcohol in a bottle and gradually add the shellac, a little at a time. Shake the bottle until all the shellac has dissolved in the liquid. Shellac varnish can be used as a diluent, but is often applied to grounds which are too absorbent, so that they will not soak up the paint. It can also be used as a fixative.

Beeswax medium
1 part white beeswax
3 parts turpentine
Put the beeswax and turpentine in a double boiler and heat gently, stirring until the beeswax is dissolved. The wax in the medium will produce a matt surface to the paint, but it can also be polished carefully to create a sheen.

Beeswax oil medium
10 parts raw linseed oil
2 parts beeswax
1/16 part litharge
Use a little of the oil and mix it with the litharge. (Take extra care when using litharge which is poisonous.) Put the rest of the oil in a metal container and warm it through slowly. Add the litharge and the beeswax in small pieces to the warm oil. This produces fumes, so work in the open or near an extractor fan. Heat the mixture to 250°C, stirring constantly. Let it cool for a while and pour it into a wide-necked container. The liquid sets hard like wax. As a medium it is useful to thicken paint for impasto techniques, or it can be added to thin paint for glazes.

Turpentine

Copal varnish

Linseed oil

Damar varnish

Mediums, solvents and diluents and varnishes A great variety of different products are now commercially available for use in the process of oil painting. Mediums are actually mixed with the paint to alter the thickness and flow of the paint, and to speed or slow the drying rate. Solvents are used to thin wet paint, and varnishes may be used as a final overall protection to the painting, or mixed with the wet paint and oil as mediums.

Copal oil mediums (**1, 2**) give the paint extra transparency and gloss. They tend to increase the drying speed. Oil vehicles (**3**) are mediums which thin the paint and improve the flow. The example shown is light and especially suited to mixing with pale colors or white. Opal medium (**4**) gives a matt effect to the paint surface and is relatively slow drying. Oil painting medium (**5**, **6**) has been specially developed as a paint thinner. It shows the least tendency to cause cracking or yellowing in the paint surface, which is always a danger when the drying process is interfered with. Liquin is also a thinner and its free flow and speed of drying make it valuable in detailed work. Turpentine (**9, 10**) and petroleum distillates (**11**) are used alone or mixed with oil and varnish to control the consistency of the wet paint. Special substances have been developed to deal with dried paint. The picture cleaner (**7**, **8**) removes dirt which has settled on a dried paint surface without disturbing the painting itself,

whereas the paint remover and solvent (**17**) is designed to soften and remove hardened color. Picture varnish (**12**) is clear and quick drying for final surface protection. Crystal damar varnish (**13**) and paper varnish (**14**) protect the paint surface with a high gloss finish. Picture mastic varnish (**15**) is also glossy but dries to a more

brittle film. Heat resisting varnish (**16**) and weather resisting varnish (**18**, **20**) have been specially developed to withstand hard conditions. The former can also be used as a medium for oil painting on china or glass. Copal varnish should be used only when the painting has completely dried out, or as a medium mixed with oil.

Retouching varnish (**22**) is a temporary varnish for newly completed work, or for use during painting. Wax varnishes (**19, 23**) give a soft sheen to the final picture. Varnish is also available in aerosol spray form (**21**) for convenience.

Oil painting Supports

Fabric

The most common supports for oil painting are fabric stretched over wooden frames, and panels of wood or wood composition. But any inert surface that can be primed and prepared to take paint will do, including cardboard, paper and even thin sheets of metal.

The term 'canvas' applies to any stretched fabric. An artist's canvas can be made from linen in several weaves; cotton and cotton weaves such as unbleached calico, duck and twill; mixed linen-cotton weaves; hessian; or man-made fibers.

Linen is considered the best canvas, with a finely-woven, knot-free linen the best of all—and the most expensive. But some artists, with revealed texture in mind, prefer a well-woven coarser weave. Cheaper linens include linen crash, which usually has knots; and linen scrim, which needs a good deal of priming because of its wide weave.

Cotton weaves stretch badly and do not prime well; but ready-primed cotton is available and, although the surface is flimsy, it may lend itself well to particular light techniques.

Wood or paper

Wood as a support has a longer history than canvas. Only that which has been properly seasoned and treated should be used or it will warp and crack. The best is mahogany. To prevent it buckling, it must be braced or cradled by wooden strips attached to the back by screws or strong adhesive.

Mahogany-faced plywood can be used, but it should not be less than five-ply—preferably eight-ply; and although it is not as liable to crack as solid wood, it should also be properly cradled.

Chipboard is made from either wood chips compressed with a resinous or oily binder, or is composed of wood fiber which needs plenty of priming. The corners and edges of chipboard tend to wear a little, but it does not warp as much as wood and needs no cradling.

Linen-cotton weaves are even less satisfactory than cotton alone. The mixed threads absorb the primer, oil and pigments to different extents and at varying rates, causing unequal tension and eventual distortion of the surface. Hessian, a very coarse jute weave, needs a good deal of priming and becomes brittle in time.

Many canvases of man-made fibers are available. Some are ready-primed with an acrylic resin. They are cheaper, lighter, clearer and more resistant to chemical action than natural fibers; but their lasting qualities, including how brittle they may become, are not yet known.

Canvases of linen or cotton weave can be bought, fully primed with size and ground, in rolls cut to any length; but many professionals prefer to prepare their own to suit their particular needs. Prepared canvas is sold in two grades: single and double primed. The double is more rigid, although not necessarily as lasting as the thinner, more pliable surface.

If the canvas is being mounted at home or in the studio, these things are necessary: stretcher or chassis, ruler, knife, a pair of canvas pliers, and either a staple gun or a hammer and tacks.

Buy stretchers with keys or tiny wedges of wood which fit into the inside angles of the corners so that the canvas can be tightened or slackened as needed. Check that the stretcher corners are securely fitted together, then make sure it is square or true. This can be done either by measuring the diagonals, which should be the same length, or by checking the inside corners with a T-square or right-angled drawing triangle. Cut the canvas with knife and ruler, allowing 1½in (3.9 cms) for overlap around the stretcher.

Lay the stretcher on the canvas—so that the weave is parallel with the sides. Fold the canvas over one side of the stretcher and staple or tack it on the inside edge of the center of the side. Then, with the pliers, stretch the canvas, fold, and repeat the central tacking or stapling in the center of the opposite side. Do this with the other two sides. Stretch and tack or staple on alternate sides, working round all four sides until the whole canvas is taut and smooth. Fold and attach the corners as flat as possible so that the mounted canvas will fit easily into a frame. If done correctly the first time, it will be unnecessary to stretch or loosen the canvas with corner keys.

There are a number of theories about protecting the back of a canvas to control or even completely to prevent moisture affecting it. Some artists completely prime it; others coat with a wax varnish, or cover it with layers of tin foil and shellac. The simplest method is to tack cardboard to the back of the stretcher so that moisure and temperature affect the canvas more slowly.

Canvas can also be 'marouflaged' on to wood or hardboard with glue or size, obviating the need for a stretcher; but for technical reasons, this is a task best left to specialists.

Muslin can be marouflaged on to chipboard with size to give a textured support. All creases must be brushed out and edges and corners pasted down and glued at the back.

Hardboard wiped with alcohol can be used unprimed, but it is better to size and prime it, treating both sides of the board at the same time to prevent it from buckling.

Laminated boards are types of heavy cardboard made from wood pulp and paper waste. They are brittle and not considered of much value as supports. Essex board, however, a laminated cardboard, makes a good support if sized on both sides. It can also be marouflaged with muslin.

Cardboard also needs sizing on both sides and should be cradled. Many artists, including Toulouse-Lautrec (1864–1901), Walter Sickert (1860–1942) and the German-born painter George Grosz (1893–1959), painted on cardboard, using the natural brown tone of the board as part of the painting.

Paper with a rough surface can be glued to hardboard and sized with casein as a support for oils. Plain, smooth paper sized with gelatin and bound into a pad is used by some artists for small paintings and color notes. Oils on paper tend to crumble and lift after a while, but there are special methods of restoring them.

Metal

Metal plates were used by the Dutch for small, finely-wrought oil paintings from the time of van Eyck. They were usually of copper. Zinc and aluminium have been tried in recent years; but ferrous–iron or steel–sheets present chemical and corrosion problems, which may have been solved for the automobile industry but not for the artist. Metal supports need no priming, but must be roughened to hold the paint.

Metal is, in fact, the only support that does not need to be separated from the oil in the grounds. Underpriming is needed for all other types of support. Oil rots the fibers of canvas after making them weak and brittle first.

Stretching a canvas 1. Fit the ends of two pieces of a stretcher together to form a corner. Fit the opposite sides and join all four.

4. Fold the overlap round the wood, and staple in the center of each side. Keeping the canvas taut, staple along the sides.

Cradling a board 1. Mitre the ends of two pieces of batten. They should be a little shorter than the width of the board.

Sticking muslin to board 1. Cut a suitable sized piece of muslin, allowing at least 2 in to overlap each side of the board.

2. Check that the assembled stretcher is square by measuring the diagonals. They should be of equal length.

5. Pull the canvas tightly across the corners diagonally, making sure it is smooth and taut on the right side. Put in a staple.

2. Drill holes for screws in the battens. Measure a position for each on the board, several inches in from the edge.

2. Lay the muslin on the board and smooth it flat. Brush over it with size to adhere it to the board, making sure no creases form.

3. Lay the stretcher on a piece of canvas and cut a rectangle at least 1½ in larger than the stretcher on all sides.

6. Fold in the remaining flaps of canvas so that the corners are neat and tight. Secure them with another two or three staples.

3. Place the battens carefully on the marked places, parallel with the short sides of the board. Screw them down firmly.

3. Turn the edges of the muslin over on to the back of the board and glue them down. Fold in the corners and glue them firmly.

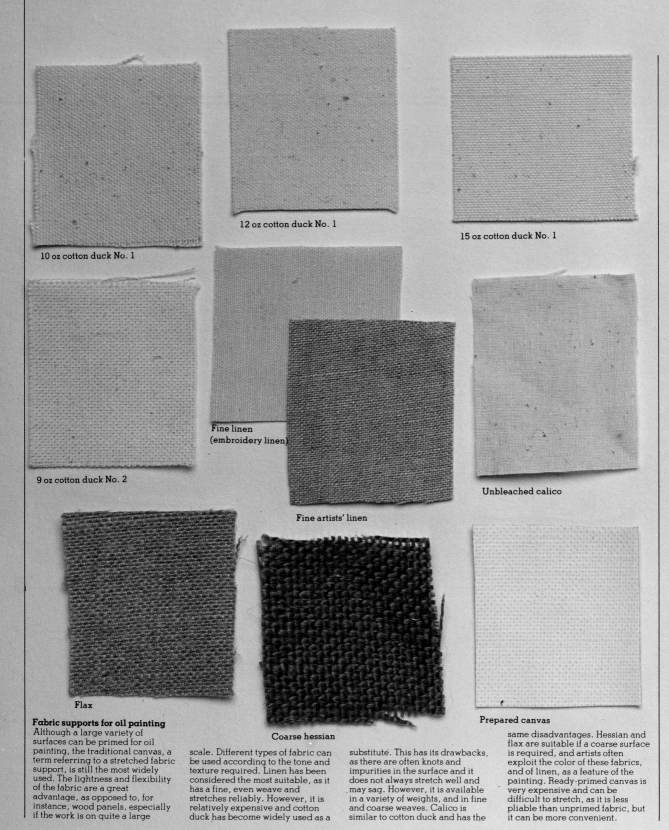

12 oz cotton duck No. 1

15 oz cotton duck No. 1

10 oz cotton duck No. 1

9 oz cotton duck No. 2

Fine linen
(embroidery linen)

Unbleached calico

Fine artists' linen

Flax

Coarse hessian

Prepared canvas

Fabric supports for oil painting
Although a large variety of
surfaces can be primed for oil
painting, the traditional canvas, a
term referring to a stretched fabric
support, is still the most widely
used. The lightness and flexibility
of the fabric are a great
advantage, as opposed to, for
instance, wood panels, especially
if the work is on quite a large

scale. Different types of fabric can
be used according to the tone and
texture required. Linen has been
considered the most suitable, as it
has a fine, even weave and
stretches reliably. However, it is
relatively expensive and cotton
duck has become widely used as a

substitute. This has its drawbacks,
as there are often knots and
impurities in the surface and it
does not always stretch well and
may sag. However, it is available
in a variety of weights, and in fine
and coarse weaves. Calico is
similar to cotton duck and has the

same disadvantages. Hessian and
flax are suitable if a coarse surface
is required, and artists often
exploit the color of these fabrics,
and of linen, as a feature of the
painting. Ready-primed canvas is
very expensive and can be
difficult to stretch, as it is less
pliable than unprimed fabric, but
it can be more convenient.

Card Most types of card, or even paper, are suitable for oil painting, provided they are well primed before the paint is applied.

Rough hardboard

Smooth hardboard

Card

Metals Since metal cannot be rotted by the paint, it does not require priming, but the surface must be roughened to provide a tooth so that the paint will adhere. Copper plates are a traditional support, but metal has not on the whole been widely used. Some metals are simply not suitable for use with paint owing to chemical changes which are liable to occur, particularly ferrous metals. An oily primer may be applied to metal if it seems necessary. A smooth surface finish can be achieved on metal.

Hardboard Either side of a piece of hardboard can be used for painting, according to whether a rough or smooth surface is required. Hardboard should be primed on both sides.

Brass

Copper

Plywood

Chipboard

Mahogany

Wood Many types of wood can be prepared as painting supports, but the main problem is the tendency of wood to warp and split. Well-seasoned hard woods, such as mahogany, are very suitable, but even these must be protected by careful priming and should be braced on the back with wood battens to prevent warping. Chipboard is more resilient and the composition is tough so it may not require extra strengthening. Plywood or blockboard can also be used, but these must be thick and solid. It is possible to join wood panels, glueing them together, but careful attention must be paid then to the direction of the grain in the different pieces, so that they are least likely to split apart through warping. The slightly rough surface of wood means that there is a suitable surface to which the ground can adhere, but if a particular texture is required on a panel, wood can be covered with canvas or muslin to obtain the effect of the weave. Wood is less suitable than canvas for use on a large scale, owing to the problems of preventing it from buckling, or of joining panels, and even quite small panels can be heavy and awkward to handle.

25

Oil painting Preparing the canvas

Size

The most common form of underpriming is that provided by a weak glue size solution. The finest but most expensive is leather waste size from the skins of animals. Bone glue size is the most commonly used.

Sprinkle bone glue into cold water and stir into a smooth paste. For every cup of powdered glue used, add seven cups of cold water, then heat the whole mixture gently until all the size is dissolved. Apply it to the canvas while it is still warm, brushing in every direction so that the size penetrates every part of the weave. When it has dried, apply a second coat.

To make size from casein glue—also known as milk glue—sprinkle the casein powder into cold water, in the proportion of one part of casein to seven of water, and stir until the casein is dissolved. Casein size must be used on the same day it is made. It resists moisture better than glue or gelatin size, but is more brittle.

Grounds

A ground forms the layer between the sizing and the paint and provides a suitable surface as well as further protecting the canvas or other support from the oil in the paint. Most grounds are white to lessen the effect of the age-darkening of the paint. Ready-prepared oil-based or acrylic-based primers can be bought for use on sized canvases.

Oil grounds should be used in two coats for the best results. An excellent ground for canvas is made from six parts of turpentine or white spirit and one part of linseed oil stirred into flake white until the mixture is thick and creamy. The second coat should be applied twelve hours or so after the first. If the ground is not dry after four to six weeks and the canvas is needed for painting, it can be given a thin coat of shellac varnish which can be painted on when dry.

Gesso grounds have been used since the Middle Ages for oil and tempera, and are still popular for tempera. Gesso can still be used for oil paintings on hardboard or wood, but it dries rigidly and in time cracks finely. Use one part of whiting to one part of heated glue size. Mix a little of the two constituents separately into a smooth paste, then add the rest of the glue and size slowly and stir until the mixture is creamy in consistency.

Emulsion grounds are a mixture of white pigment suspended in size and oil. Emulsion dries quickly—a canvas coated with it can be used after a week—is more absorbent than an oil ground and more flexible than gesso. It will also take pigment for those who want to work on a tinted ground. Mix one part of whiting with one part of zinc oxide and one part of hot glue size. Use only a portion of the size to make a paste and into this mixture slowly beat a half-part of linseed oil drop by drop until it has completely dispersed. Then add the remainder of the hot size. Keep the ground heated in a double boiler and apply it while it is still warm.

Acrylic grounds are now available for both oils and acrylics and can be applied directly on to the support without size. They have been in use for some twenty years and have not yet shown any major disadvantages.

Ingredients for grounds There are two stages of applying a ground for an oil painting, first the sizing of the raw canvas, then a thick layer of priming, which is applied in two or three thin coats. The following ingredients are used in sizing and for the preparation of various primers: turpentine, linseed oil, Gilder's whiting, flake white, or other white pigment, glue size crystals, zinc oxide. The ground serves to protect the canvas from the oil and provides a smooth, fresh surface for painting. As long as the canvas or other support is properly protected, the thickness and smoothness of the ground are a matter of personal choice. Although it is usual to apply white grounds, it is possible to add colored pigment if a colored ground is required, or to paint a thin layer of color over the dry ground. The powder ingredients in general add body to the mixture and make it opaque. The white pigment adds brilliance to the whiteness of the ground. Powdered ingredients must be kept dry in order to mix smoothly.

Turpentine

Recipes for preparing grounds

Various types of grounds can be made from the ingredients shown. A ground which contains oil will be less brittle when it dries than one made only from size and powder. A higher proportion of powder in the mixture will make it thicker and less flexible in application. From the materials shown here, all three types of grounds for oil painting can be made — oil ground, gesso ground and emulsion ground. Priming layers should always be applied in successive, thin coats rather than one thick layer, otherwise they will crack severely while drying and the paint will not adhere.

Glue size

1 cup glue size crystals
7 cups water
Sprinkle the glue size into the water and stir. Heat the glue in a double boiler, until all the size has dissolved, but do not allow it to boil. Apply the size to the canvas while warm.

Oil ground

6 parts turpentine
1 part linseed oil
A quantity of flake white powder
Mix the turpentine and linseed oil together and gradually pour them into the flake white, stirring continuously until the mixture is of a thick, creamy consistency. Apply in two thin coats, allowing the first to dry out before applying the second.

Gesso ground

1 part Gilder's whiting
1 part glue size
Heat the glue size gently. Add some of the warm size to the whiting and stir until it forms a thick paste. Gradually add the rest of the size until a smooth, creamy mixture is obtained. Apply gesso carefully in thin layers, or it will crack. To increase the brilliance of the white, add white powdered pigment.

Emulsion ground

1 part Gilder's whiting
1 part zinc oxide
1 part glue size
½ part linseed oil
Add part of the glue size to the whiting and zinc oxide and mix it into a paste. Add the linsed oil one drop at a time and beat it into the mixture. Mix in the rest of the glue size and keep the whole mixture warm in a double boiler until use.

Applying size and ground to a canvas 1. Heat size in a double boiler and brush it on the canvas, working well into the weave.

2. When the size is dry apply the white ground in an even coat. Do not lay it too thickly. Let it dry out, and apply another coat.

Staining a white ground 1. Mix up paint with plenty of turpentine in a tin or jar. Make enough to cover the whole canvas.

2. Brush the paint generously over the white ground so that the surface is completely covered with wet color.

3. Wipe the canvas with a dry rag to soak up the excess paint, leaving a stain of color. Repeat as necessary.

Linseed oil

Flake white powder pigment

Gilder's whiting

Glue size crystals

Zinc oxide

Oil painting Equipment

Paints

Two grades of ready-made oil paints are sold: those labelled 'Artists' and a cheaper kind, called 'Students', or by some trade name. The cheaper contain lower-quality pigments and may be less permanent.

In general, the same pigments are used in oils as in watercolors, gouache, tempera and acrylics. Only three pigments are comparatively unaffected by conditions which alter the properties of other pigments: heat, light, moisture, acidity or alkalinity. These are carbon black, cobalt and viridian.

Most permanent are the earth colors such as yellow ochre, terre verte, raw and burnt sienna, raw and burnt umber, light red, Indian red, Venetian red and natural ultramarine. These are natural earths. Artificial mineral pigments include aureolin, the cadmiums, viridian and cobalt blue. Organic pigments are divided into animal: sepia, carmine, Indian yellow; vegetable: gamboge, the madders, sap green, indigo; and artificial: Prussian blue. It is vital to use good quality whites, as nearly all colors are mixed with them.

Most pigments are susceptible to chemical interactions and atmospheric conditions. Lead white, for instance, a metal-based pigment, can be discolored by sulphur fumes in the air. Ageing oil yellows, and can turn chrome yellow into a green. Strong sunlight darkens madder, sepia and carmine. Metal-based pigments blacken if mixed with sulphides such as the cadmiums; and should not be mixed with certain synthetics, including vermilion and ultramarine.

Many made-up paints contain an excess of oil to increase their shelf life; and although this can be removed by placing the paint on an absorbent surface, many artists prefer to make up at least some of their colors from scratch, adding just as much or as little oil as they need, experimenting with textures and direct blending of pigments.

Raw pigments can be bought at most artists' supply stores, together with the equipment for home mixing: a glass slab or old litho stone, a glass miller or muller and a palette knife or spatula. Pour enough binder on the powdered pigment on the glass to make it glutinous and blend it with the palette knife. Stir the paint with a circular motion until it is of an even consistency, exerting pressure with the glass muller. The paint can be stored in a glass jar, covering it with water if it is to be kept for long.

Brushes

Oil painting brushes are usually of bleached hogs' hair and red sable hair. The making of good quality brushes, even on a mass production basis, is a skilled craft. A brushmaker will never trim the painting ends of the brushes, but will shuffle and arrange the hairs or bristles and adjust them within the metal grip or ferrule to give the right shape, even utilizing the natural curve of some bristles so that they form a gentle curve inwards instead of splaying out.

Hogs' bristle has split ends, which help hold the paint to the brush; and this is reckoned an advantage over sable brushes which, nevertheless, give a smoother stroke and find a place in any good collection of brushes. They are generally thinner and smaller.

The basic brush shapes are bright, round, flat and filbert. Brights are short-bristled with square ends; rounds are round and round-ended, good for thin paint; flats are similar to brights but with longer bristles, giving a longer stroke; filberts are similar to rounds but wider; 'longs' in sable oil brushes are similar to bristle flats; chisel edges, good for painting straight edges, are not often seen today.

Wide, supple badger blenders, made from badger hair, are used to take out brush strokes or blend wet areas into each other. Wipe them often on absorbent cloth when employing this technique. Fan brushes of red sable are used for the same purpose as badger blenders but give a softer effect.

Brushes should be cleaned immediately after each day's use. First rinse them in turpentine or white spirit and wipe them dry, or shake them in warm water with a strong household soap and wash the soap off thoroughly under warm running water.

Brushes which have been caked with paint for a long time can be cleaned with paint stripper, but this shortens their lives. Never leave a brush soaking with the bristles or hairs touching the sides or bottom of the container.

Other oil painting equipment

Knives Palette knives, made from smooth flexible steel, come in many shapes and sizes and are used for mixing the paint on the palette; painting knives, with thin, delicate blades and often longer handles, are used to apply paint directly to the canvas.

Palettes Palettes can be oval or rectangular and made of wood, china or glass. Palettes with thumb holes are made for easel painting; but, in the studio, palettes of almost any non-porous material can be placed handily on a nearby steady surface.

Treat new wooden palettes with linseed oil to prevent the wood feeding on the oil in the paint. Disposable paper palettes, with paint-proof peel-off sheets, are now made.

Dippers Dippers are small open-topped cans made to hold oil and turpentine and clip on to the edge of the palette. But in the studio it may be more convenient to use containers resting on a nearby steady surface.

Mahl sticks A mahl stick is traditionally a cane with a chamois tip which rests on the canvas to steady the painting arm. Some are now made of aluminium with a rubber tip and come in 12, 24, and 36in sizes. But they are easy to make by tying a bundle of rags to the end of a garden cane.

Easels Easels vary greatly in size and weight. The most comfortable is the traditional artist's donkey, a studio easel at which the artist can work sitting down; but the simplest kind of radial easel is substantial enough for most needs. It has short tripod legs and the upright column can be tilted and fixed by a screw, while the tray and top grip for the stretcher or board slide up and down the column.

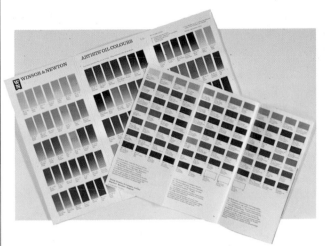

Paint and palettes

Although commercially available tube paints are a relatively recent development in the history of oil painting, the researches of color chemists since the nineteenth century have provided an enormous range of colors for contemporary artists, from both natural and synthetic pigments. The type of pigment affects the cost of the paint and charts produced by manufacturers (**above**) generally code the colors to indicate the price, and also include notes on the permanence of colors. So very many colors can be bought that it is now less common to find that artists have mixed their own paint from basic ingredients, but this may still be necessary where a specific color or paint quality is required.

The traditional oil painter's palette is a flat piece of wood with a thumbhole and indentation at one end for the fingers (**4**, **8**). These are intended for easel painters, so that the full range of color can be laid out and held ready while working. Small dippers (**5**) can be attached to the palette with clips to hold oil or turpentine. Palette boxes (**1**, **2**) are useful for outdoor work and oil sketching, as they can be closed up and carried with the colors still in place. Recessed palettes are available in plastic (**3**), aluminium (**7**) and china and may be useful for mixing thin paint for glazes. Paper palettes (**6**) are disposable and can be torn off as they are used to save cleaning. For studio use, a large sheet of glass or wood may be all that is required

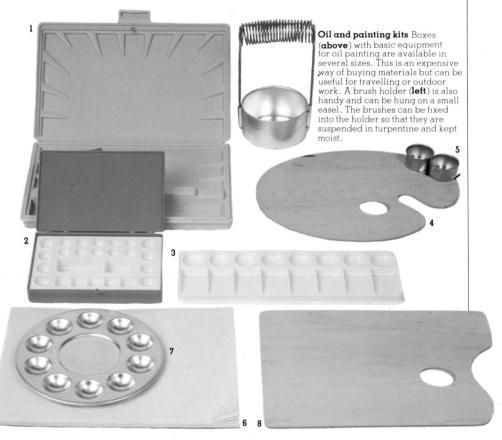

Oil and painting kits Boxes (**above**) with basic equipment for oil painting are available in several sizes. This is an expensive way of buying materials but can be useful for travelling or outdoor work. A brush holder (**left**) is also handy and can be hung on a small easel. The brushes can be fixed into the holder so that they are suspended in turpentine and kept moist.

29

Brushes for oil painting

The three basic shapes of oil
brushes are shown **above.** Flat
brushes (**left**) are very versatile, as
broad strokes can be made with
the flat of the brush, or fine lines
and dabs of paint with the tips or
side of the bristles. Filbert brushes
(center) are shaped slightly at the
tip to produce a smooth, rounded
stroke. Round hair brushes (**right**)
are useful for applying thin paint
and for covering large areas
which contain no detail.
There are a number of different
types of brushes (**right**) which vary
according to the type of hair used
for the bristles and the overall
size. Hogs' hair or sable are the
best bristles, but many different
synthetic materials have been
developed for brushes which are
often perfectly adequate. Flat
brushes may be made with long
bristles, or with shorter hairs in
which case they are known as
brights. The examples shown here
are: (from **top** to **bottom**) red sable
bright, synthetic flat, Russian
sable bright, hogs' hair filbert,
hogs' hair flat, synthetic bright,
synthetic round, red sable round,
red sable fan blender. Fan brushes
are made for one purpose. The
splayed bristles make it easy to
feather wet paint and blend
colors together. The strength of
hogs' hair makes it more suitable
than sable for applying large areas
of thick paint quickly; but if
detailed work is to be done, sable
is better because a point can be
obtained. Hogs' hair is too stiff and
thick to make a real point.
Synthetics vary in quality, but
some have the advantage of being
quite firm, but less coarse than
hogs' hair. Flat brushes, carefully
handled, can be ideal for working
into a definite outline, as they do
not splay out so much under
pressure as round brushes. In this
respect also, brights may be easier
to control than flat brushes with
long bristles. To lay paint with a
smooth, flat surface, the brush
should be handled firmly while
applying the paint, but then used
lightly in all directions to feather
over the surface and remove
brushmarks.

Mahl stick and palette knives A mahl stick (**1**) is a useful aid in painting and can be bought ready made, or assembled from easily obtained materials. It is used as a rest for the hand which holds the brush, to steady it when painting details, and consists of a length of bamboo or dowling with a cushion at one end. The stick is held across the canvas with the cushioned end resting lightly on the painting. Care must be taken not to mark the canvas by pressing too hard. Palette knives have several uses. As the name implies, they were principally used to mix up color on the palette, but they are a good alternative to brushes for certain techniques, such as impasto, and may be used to scrape away wet paint when making alterations to the picture. The particular uses of the different shapes and sizes are to some extent a matter of the painter's own preference. The broad, rounded blades (**2**, **6**) are flexible along the whole length and exert the necessary pressure for mixing the colors on the palette. The long side of these knives can be used to scrape away wet paint without damaging the ground or the canvas. Painting knives with small, angular blades (**3**, **4**, **5**) are used to apply and shape small dabs or broad sweeps of paint to the canvas. A plastic palette knife (**7**) is also useful.

Brush sizes Brushes are produced in series, a range of sizes in which the composition of the brush remains the same. As shown here, for instance, a series of round hogs' hair brushes may be produced in twelve sizes, the smallest numbered 1, and so on up to the largest, 12. This applies to all shapes of brushes and types of bristles. A painter may prefer to use only one shape of brush, perhaps filberts, and will then require several different sizes. On the other hand, if all types of brushes are used, only three sizes of each may be necessary, small, medium and large. Large sable brushes can be extremely expensive, and it may be preferable to find a substitute. The type of brush needed will obviously also depend upon the style of the work and could be quite limited. A useful, all-purpose range of brushes might contain two or three sizes of each.

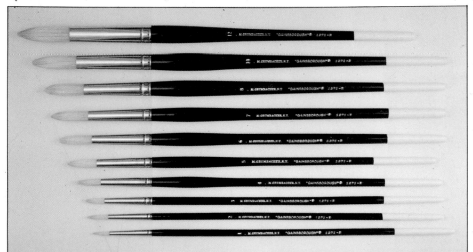

Easels for oils Easels provide a firm support for painting. A good easel is therefore an essential piece of equipment for all artists, including the beginner. A wide selection of easels is available to suit the artist's needs. Modern easels vary considerably in size, weight and style. Easels that are permanently in a studio tend to be heavy and made of a durable hardwood such as beech. They should be positioned carefully in a studio to receive the best possible light. If the studio is small, consider buying a collapsible easel which may be stored away when not in use. Lightweight aluminium easels provide an alternative to sturdy wooden ones. They are inexpensive, but they are

not as stable as wooden easels. Portable folding easels are convenient for work done outside the studio. The combination sketch box-easel-canvas carrier (**1**), made from a seasoned hardwood, is very compact and weighs only 13 lbs when empty. This makes it suitable for artists who travel or who do not have a large studio. By unfolding the legs, the sketch box is quickly converted into an easel. The legs should be adjusted to the desired height and position. The canvas carrier section of the easel should also be set at a convenient angle at a comfortable height. There is a useful drawer in the easel where paints and brushes may be kept. Another popular easel is the

traditional artist's donkey (**3**). This is a large easel that incorporates a bench. Although it takes up a good deal of space, it is often used by artists who prefer to work sitting down. It is particularly used for detail work which can be tiring if done standing up. The angle of the easel can be adjusted readily and the drawing board or canvas held firm by wooden sliding blocks. A table easel (**4**) can be used on a low table or on a high chair. This is a handy easel that is compact when folded for carrying or storage. It can be adjusted either backwards or forwards to a working angle. For outdoor work a collapsible easel (**5**) is required. This model has telescopic legs that are easily adjusted to the right height. Although it is fairly light, it

provides a firm support. A larger
easel that is good for indoor work
is the radial easel (**7**). This can be
tilted backwards and forwards as
required during work. One of the
advantages of this easel is that it
may be folded up when not in use.
A studio easel (**6**) is essential for
artists who work on large
canvases. If necessary, a very
wide canvas may be supported by
two of these easels (**2**). The hinged
upright frame may be adjusted so
that the canvas is raised over three
feet from the ground. The holding
frame may also be tilted forwards
or backwards from the vertical to
suit the artist. A studio easel is not
convenient for working with small
canvases. It is heavy, takes up a lot
of room and is not collapsible.

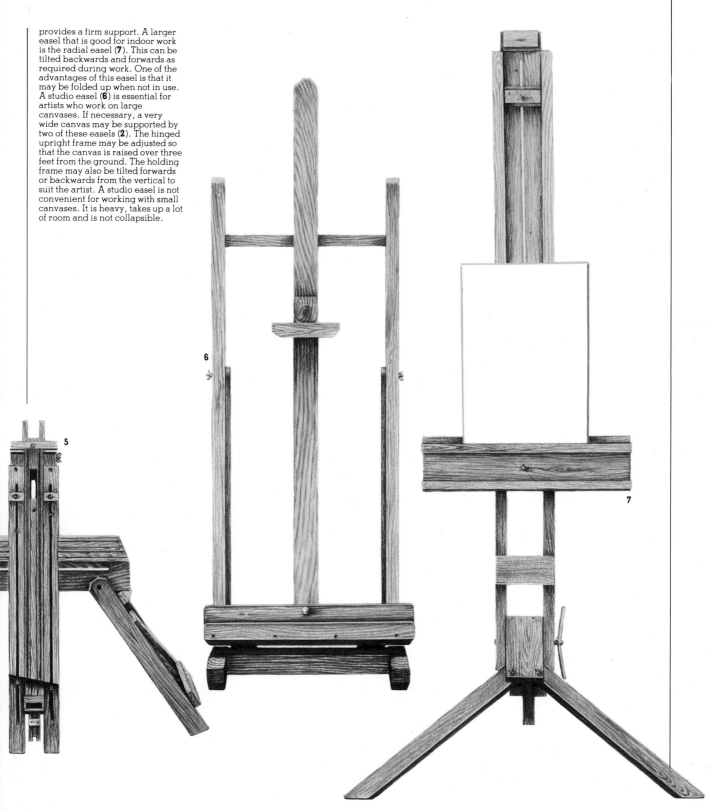

Oil painting Techniques

Every artist develops a personal style in time, after mastering his or her chosen medium, and today's painters are fortunate in having the wealth of the past, conveyed in modern color reproduction, over which to ponder and consider along what paths their own stylistic leanings and aesthetic values may lead them.

In very broad terms, there are two contrasting types of oil painting; the carefully considered work, built up slowly over weeks, months or even years; and the *alla prima* type, in which the artist is concerned with directly conveying a first impression of the subject, usually in a single session, without a preliminary drawing stage.

Titian used this direct method, applying his color immediately without any preliminary sketching: drawing, so to speak, as he painted. Michelangelo was slyly derogatory about this method, saying that it was a pity the Venetians did not start painting by learning to draw first. Velasquez also liked to work *alla prima*.

One of the main features of modern *alla prima* painting is the wet-into-wet technique. While the first layer is still wet, the artist paints or scumbles into it, at times making the colors deliberately run into each other. This technique is clearly shown in *The Fifer* by Edouard Manet (1832–1883) in the Jeu de Paume Museum in Paris. Flat areas of color are thrown into contrast by the impasto on sash and spats.

Monet was a leading exponent of *alla prima* painting. Like van Gogh, he took his canvases to his subjects, often outdoors, and painted rapidly with little or no underpainting. Sisley, Gauguin and Cézanne used solid strokes of opaque color with the many variations of scumbles and glazes and transparencies. Even Turner, long before the Impressionists, realized the advantages of *alla prima* as can be seen in his fluid preliminary landscape studies. The British artist L. S. Lowry (1887–1976) sometimes blended thick colors while they were still wet, as in his *Yachts at Lytham*.

'Frottage' on oils is another wet technique started by Max Ernst (1891–1976). It is a method of forming an uneven texture on wet, flat opaque color. A sheet of non-absorbent paper is put over it, gently pressed on to the paint, then peeled away.

Planned and pre-drawn oil painting goes back to van Eyck. Other major practitioners include Rubens, David, Turner, Degas and Salvador Dali. These artists sketched their designs first, either with charcoal washed over with a thin glaze which still showed the lines; or painted on with thin brush strokes.

Some artists draw a whole sketch separately and then transfer it to the canvas by squaring-up: drawing a squared grid on the original sketch, then a respectively-sized grid on to the canvas. Then they copy the picture in each sketch square on to the canvas.

Underpainting is a method of putting down neutral tones and colors in lean paint as part of the design to form a basis for light and shaded overpainting.

Rembrandt and the grisaille painters who followed him underpainted in grays and whites overlaid with thin glazes, with dark tones for shadows also glazed over.

Glazes reflect light from the color beneath them, giving a painting a glowing, three-dimensional quality. The medium should contain beeswax in preference to linseed oil, which tends to move. Glazes can be laid over underpaint, impastos, or opaque paint. Titian and El Greco (1541–1614) painted lustrous rich red tapestries by using glazes over underpaint and impasto.

'Impasto' is thick paint applied with a knife or brush to give a three-dimensional effect. It is mainly used under glazes, but some painters have made whole pictures from impastos, giving a rich-textured effect. Impasto is best mixed with a resinous medium.

Scumbling is the application of opaque paint over darker opaque paint in an uneven manner so that the paint underneath shows through. It can be brushed on in a circular motion, dabbed, stippled, smudged or streaked. Scumbling can also be done with the edge of the hand, the fingers, or a cloth.

It is not vital to varnish all oil paintings. Most will not suffer if hung in reasonable conditions; and varnish does tend to yellow with age. However, if varnishing must be done to protect the painting, wait for six months or so until the paint is really dry. For a glossy finish, use a soft resin or spirit varnish; for a slightly matt surface, use a wax varnish.

Squaring up 1. Draw a light grid of squares over a drawing. Place the drawing on an easel beside the canvas.

3. Draw in the basic outlines of the composition using the grid as a guide. Work until there is enough detail to start painting.

2. Mark out on the canvas a grid proportionate — either enlarged or reduced — to the grid on the drawing.

Underpainting 1. Using paint well thinned with turpentine, start to lay in basic areas of tone and work the color into the canvas weave.

2. Continue working over the area with the thinned paint, following the drawn outlines so that the main shapes begin to emerge.

3. The colors underneath glow through the glaze but the hues are modified. Allow each layer to dry fully before adding more glaze.

Glazing over impasto 1. Lay thick paint with a knife, making a coarse, craggy texture. Leave it until the surface has dried out.

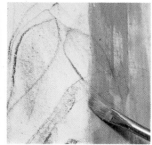

3. Block in large areas of basic tone with thinned paint in a neutral color. Let the drawing show through the paint.

3. Use thinned paint in another color to provide darker areas of tone and start to work in the detailed shapes.

Glazing over oil crayon.
1. Draw directly on the canvas with oil crayons, varying the thickness of the marks.

2. Mix up thin paint for glazing, brush lightly over the impasto paint and let it settle into the pitted surface.

4. Use thicker paint to establish the main colors and basic shapes.

Glazing 1. Mix paint for glazing with a medium, not with turpentine alone, so that it has a thin but oily consistency.

2. Mix up a quantity of paint thinned with medium to make a transparent glaze. Paint lightly over the crayoned area.

Underdrawing with charcoal
1. Draw out the composition quite freely with charcoal using line and tone; correct as necessary.

5. Gradually obliterate the drawing as the painting develops.

2. Apply the glaze in a thin layer over the dried underpainting to form a transparent film of color.

3. Thick areas of crayon show clearly through the thin paint. Light areas of crayon form a textured sheen underneath.

2. Dust the drawing over lightly with a clean rag before starting to paint, to remove charcoal dust from the canvas.

Making a mahl stick 1. Cut two small grooves around a piece of dowling 3 feet long, about 1 inch from the end.

2. Fit absorbent cotton on the end of the dowling. Tease it out so that it forms a soft knob over the cut end.

3. Wrap a clean piece of cloth over absorbent cotton and tie with string so that the grooves hold it firmly. Trim the cloth.

4. To use the mahl stick, rest the soft end gently on the canvas or edge of the stretcher and steady the brush hand on the stick.

Scraping back and wiping 1. To retrieve the surface for repainting, scrape back paint from the canvas with a palette knife.

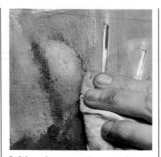

2. Wipe the scraped area with a rag soaked in turpentine. Clean away as much paint as possible from the canvas.

Painting wet into wet 1. Lay a patch of color. While it is wet work into it with a second color and blend together.

2. Work in another color and blend it into the others, making a range of tones develop. Keep the paint wet and brush into it loosely.

3. Add more paint until the required effect is achieved. Lay in more color to redefine the tones if necessary.

Blending with a fan brush 1. Paint stripes of different tones of one color side by side on the canvas.

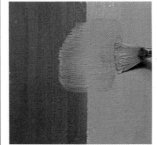

2. Brush lightly with the fan brush over the line where two colors meet. Wipe surplus paint off the brush while working.

3. Continue to work across the bands of color until they are all blended together smoothly and no harsh lines are visible.

4. The completed area shows a soft progression through the tonal range. Use a fan brush also to blend different hues.

Brushmarks 1. The mark left by a brush depends on its shape and the hair from which it is made. This is a hogs' hair filbert.

2. This chisel-shaped brush is also made of hogs' hair. Hogs' hair has a split end which helps hold the paint.

3. The main brush shapes are bright, flat, round and filbert. This hogs' hair brush is a round.

4. This smaller round brush is made of sable. Use this brush to touch in small areas. Sable gives a smooth, soft stroke.

5. This small hogs' hair filbert is useful for making long tapering strokes. Filberts curve gently to a point at the top.

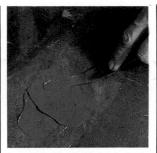

2. Clean the bristles with soap under running water. Work the soap well into the brush to remove all the color, rinse well.

Impasto with a knife 1. Mix thick paint on the palette with a knife, add medium if necessary to give the paint extra body.

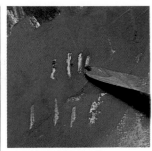

Scratched textures 1. Lay an area of thick paint and while it is wet, scrape away small marks with the end of a palette knife.

6. This large hogs' hair chisel is being used to allow the paint to dribble.

Impasto with a brush 1. Mix up thick paint on the palette, adding only enough turpentine to make it malleable.

2. Scoop up a generous amount of paint on the knife and spread it on the canvas. Work it into broad, textured ridges.

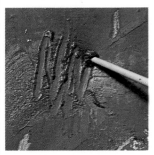

2. Use a stick or the wood end of a brush to scratch into thick, wet paint, as if drawing. A variety of marks can be made this way.

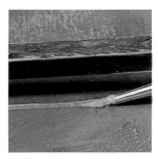

7. A fine sable brush like this can be used with a ruler. Any artist needs a selection of brush sizes and shapes.

2. Load the brush with paint and apply it thickly to the canvas in short, heavy strokes, leaving brush marks.

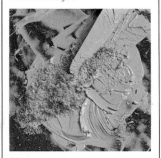

Mixing sawdust with paint 1. Lay out paint and sawdust on the palette and mix them well together.

Scumbling Load the brush with fairly dry paint and dab lightly with the brush, making an area of broken color.

Cleaning a brush 1. Rinse the brush in a jar of turpentine and wipe it thoroughly with a rag.

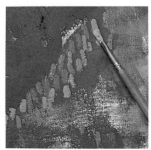

3. Build up an impasto layer with small, thick dabs of different colors. The brushmarks help to describe form and texture.

2. The textured paint should be thick but not too dry. Spread it over the canvas, work it into the weave to make it adhere.

Frottage with flat paper 1. Using paint thinned with oil and turpentine, lay an area of flat color.

2. Lay a sheet of paper over the paint and press it down gently. Rub lightly over the paper with the fingertips.

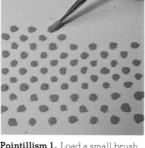

Pointillism 1. Load a small brush with paint and, using the tip of the brush, make a pattern of regular dots.

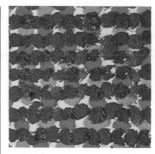

5. Work over again in a fourth color. The number of colors which can be used is virtually unlimited.

3. Repeat the stencilling with a different shape and color. Be careful, if overlapping shapes, not to disturb the color beneath.

3. Peel the paper away. It lifts some of the paint to form a textured surface. Experiment until you get the right effect.

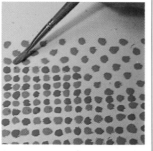

2. Work over the area with dots of another color. Keep the colors separate at this stage and do not let them overlap.

6. Different stages of the process show how the colors are successively modified. At a distance, the colors merge.

4. Bought stencils can be used for letter forms and figures. You can cut any shape required from stencil film or thin card.

Frottage with crumped paper 1. Crumple paper into a tight ball and open it out carefully. Press the paper into a patch of wet paint.

3. Add a third color. Start gradually to cover the white space and let the dots begin to join up and overlap.

Stencilling 1. Hold the stencil firmly against the canvas and dab on fairly dry paint with the flat of the brush bristles.

Varnishing Apply varnish evenly with the brush held almost flat to the canvas. Oils should dry for some months before varnishing.

2. Peel the paper back from the paint. If it has not lifted enough paint, repeat the process with a clean piece of paper.

4. To alter the impression of the spotted area, change the relationships of warm and cold hues and light and dark tones.

2. Peel back the stencil carefully and check that the painted shape is clean. If the paint is too wet the edges will blur.

Acrylics.

Development and characteristics. Surfaces: Canvas, Wood, Metals, Paper and card, Murals. **Paint and equipment. Techniques:** Glazes, Flat color, Brushing, Hard edge design and drawing with line, Impasto, Airbrushing, Cleaning, Varnishing.

Acrylics Development, characteristics

Paints comprising pigment bound in a synthetic resin are usually known as acrylics. Even if the resin is not an acrylic but a polyvinyl acetate, for example, the paints are still loosely referred to as acrylics.

Acrylic paint in art developed from the need to combat atmospheric conditions. Artists working in Mexico in the 1920s found that oil paint and even fresco was not sufficiently durable in a permanently exposed position. For work such as murals they required a paint which would dry quickly and remain stable under all weather conditions.

Notable pioneers of the use of acrylics in art were painter and illustrator José Clemente Orozco (1883–1949), Diego Rivera (1886–1957), noted for his murals, and David Alfaro Siqueiros (1896–1974). Siqueiros delivered a paper on *The Mexican Experiment in Art* as a delegate to the American Artists' Congress in New York. Shortly afterwards, in 1936, he established an experimental workshop, named after him, where artists studied the new medium of acrylics.

Almost every traditional method of art is still being used today, but until acrylics first appeared artists had used the same materials for over 400 years. At first painters used acrylics similarly to traditional media, but it was not long before they exploited the special characteristics and extended their use far beyond exterior murals.

Acrylics resemble watercolor, gouache and tempera in body and substance of color. They dry to an even, matt finish. Acrylic paints are emulsions and can be diluted with acrylic media or water or both. Their great advantage is that, although they can be diluted with water, they dry within minutes and once dry do not change in color or texture. The surface is sealed, and the artist can either lay more paint or a glaze over the top without either coat altering, each layer being sufficiently porous to allow total evaporation and of such adhesive strength as to form almost indestructible strata. The paints resist chemical decomposition and oxydization. Both acrylic paint and PVA are stable, do not reflect light and are opaque, although they can be diluted to obtain transparency. Rapid drying can be halted by adding a proprietary retarder or pure glycerin to the paint on the palette.

By the 1950s acrylic paints were on sale in the United States and being widely used by such artists as Jackson Pollock (1912–1956), Mark Rothko (1903–1970), Kenneth Noland (born 1929) and Robert Motherwell (born 1913). Much of their work was abstract or Pop in form. Pollock was much influenced by Orozco's expressionism and by the techniques of the Surrealists in the 1940s. Pollock often poured paint on to a canvas on the floor and he used many glazes and impastos. Noland uses solid areas of opaque color which have hard edges.

It was not until the 1960s that acrylic paints were widely available in Britain. They are now used by such well-known British artists as David Hockney (born 1937), Leonard Rosoman (born 1912), Bridget Riley (born 1931), Peter Blake (born 1932) and Tom Phillips (born 1937).

Acrylics Paint and equipment

A selection of the basic colors, not necessarily more than 15, can provide a wide range of colors and tones. Winsor and Newton's Liquitex and Aqua-Tec encompass a wide choice as does Rowney's Cryla. Although PVA colors are cheaper, they lack permanence. A basic palette would include black, white, lemon yellow, yellow ochre, raw sienna, Venetian red, cadmium red, deep violet, cerulean blue, cobalt blue, ultramarine, Hooker's green, monastral green and bright green. As a result of laboratory research new colors such as phthalocyanine green and dioxazine purple are available as well as the traditional colors. The nozzle of the tube of paint must be cleaned after use and before replacing the cap to prevent air penetrating and solidifying the contents.

Gouache colors, available from Rowney, can be mixed with acrylic medium on the palette, allowing layers of paint to be laid over each other without the color underneath being affected—which ordinary gouache will not do. Medium is added to the paint as described in this chapter in the section on glazes.

Apart from the materials described in connection with each technique, equipment for painting with acrylics, such as knives, easels, palettes and drawing-boards, is common to oil and water-color painting. It is usually easier, however, to clean acrylic paint from white plastic palettes than from wood. Sable water-color brushes are best if using diluted acrylic for fine work. Acrylic paint dries so hard so quickly that brushes must be thoroughly washed of all pigment in warm water immediately after use. A completely solid brush can be soaked in methylated spirits for about 12 hours; the paint can then be worked out between the fingers and the brush washed immediately in a mixture of soap and water.

Airbrushes must be cleaned thoroughly and the parts checked regularly to ensure that they have not worked loose. Spitting could mean that the needle is stuck on a coarse particle of pigment or that the paint needs thinning. If the paint comes out irregularly it could be that the needle is out of place or fitted too tightly, the nozzle is worn, or the pigment has dried in the nozzle's fluid passage; the latter requires the nozzle to be soaked for a long time and cleaned. A bent needle or an obstruction in the air cap can cause a lop-sided spray. The nozzle cap can cause the paint to build up; it should be cleaned either by removing it and placing the tip flat on a piece of paper and blowing, or by unscrewing it and cleaning it inside and out with a stiff brush, a damp lint-free cloth or a toothpick.

Acrylic paints, mediums, varnishes Rowney Cryla (**2**) is just one example of the wide range of a acrylic paints on sale today. Grumbacher, and Winsor and Newton manufacture similar ranges. The liquid texture of Rowney Flow Formula (**1**) is used for covering large areas with flat color. The canvas should be primed with an acrylic primer (**3**) or gesso (**4**). Mediums are available in gloss (**5**, **7**, **11**, **13**) or matt (**6**, **10**) textures. Retarding medium (**16**) slows the drying time of the paint. Like mediums, varnishes can be matt (**8**, **9**) or gloss. Acrylic varnishes are normally insoluble, but Rowney make a soluble gloss variety (**12**). Also useful are gel medium (**15**) and water tension breaker (**14**).

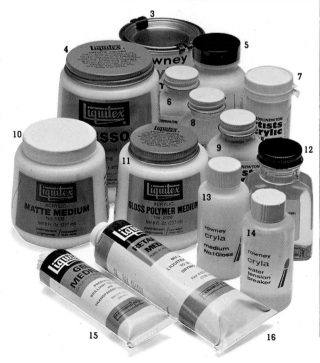

Mixing tube paint with medium
1. Squeeze out some paint on to the palette and drop in a quantity of the medium.

2. Mix with a brush. Medium can give the paint a matt or gloss finish. Thin with water if required. Mix two colors like this also.

Making up acrylic paint 1. Large quantities of paint can be mixed up using raw acrylic medium, gel and powder or liquid pigments.

2. To make the gel, pour the liquid acrylic medium into a large container and slowly add the thickening agent.

3. Stir the mixture vigorously as it begins to gel. Do not add too much thickening agent. Let it stand for 8-12 hours to gel.

4. To mix the paint, place the powder pigment on the palette and pour on the liquid acrylic medium. Mix them with a knife.

5. Add a few drops of water, mix in the gel gradually until the paint is the right consistency.

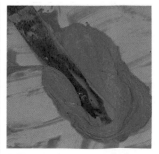

6. The mixed paint has a thick, smooth consistency but can be thinned with water as required.

Acrylics Surfaces

Acrylic paint can be laid on almost any practical support. A ground is not necessary, but an acrylic primer is generally used. This is an acrylic medium mixed with inert titanium white, and two or three thin coats are usually applied. Unprimed surfaces dry to a matt finish. Paint on a primed surface produces a slight gloss, but this can be prevented by adding water to the paint. Oil-primed canvas cannot be used for acrylic paints; nor are ordinary emulsion grounds compatible with acrylic. Polymer primer is often referred to as polymer gesso, but it is not a real chalk-glue mixture gesso which is fully absorbent.

Canvas

All types of canvas are good supports for acrylics, and glue size is not required. When stretching unprimed canvas a little slack should be allowed, because the primer or paint makes it contract and become taut. If a canvas such as hessian with a very coarse weave is being used, an acrylic medium is required; the two chief types are the standard or gloss and the matt. The latter can be used as a final protective coat. Both can be used without water. There are also glaze media which produce a transparent effect.

Wood

Acrylic paints and wooden panels combine well; natural wood, plywood, compressed woods, block-boards and hardboard can be used. Hardboard must be cradled at the back to prevent buckling; its smooth side should be sanded and an acrylic primer applied before painting.

Metals

Copper and zinc are the most suitable metals for acrylic paints. Coarse sanding and an application of primer is recommended.

Paper and card

Acrylics can be painted on almost any card and heavy paper, whether primed or unprimed. Paper may buckle under the weight of the primer, and it should therefore be stretched over a frame if big washes of paint are contemplated.

Murals

External walls usually require some preparation, but acrylic paints are particularly suitable since they weather better than oils and do not reflect light. Plaster should be sanded smooth before priming or painting.

Preparing surfaces for acrylic paint Acrylic paint can be used on a wide variety of surfaces, but it is important to prepare the surface correctly. If a primer is used, it must be of the acrylic variety; ordinary primer will not bind with acrylic paint. Acrylic primer is a mixture of acrylic medium and titanium white. Ready-made varieties are not expensive. It is best to coat the surface carefully and evenly with two or three coats, allowing each to dry thoroughly before the next is applied. A primed surface will dry to a slightly egg-shell gloss finish, while an unprimed, absorbent surface will dry to give an even matt finish, because the surface absorbs the pigment.

Staining raw canvas 1. Thin the paint so that it is liquid and wipe it evenly over the canvas weave, using a sponge.

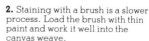

2. Staining with a brush is a slower process. Load the brush with thin paint and work it well into the canvas weave.

3. A canvas may be stained evenly in one color, or with different patches of color. These will mix where they overlap.

Acrylics Techniques

Acrylic paints have a transparency which is similar to watercolor in that a white ground will shine through a color without needing further white overpainting. The paints take on a transparency when mixed with water or acrylic medium.

Glazes

Acrylic paint for glazing, mixed with water or glaze medium, is used in the initial stages of the painting. Medium is added to paint on the palette by dripping a little into a well made in a small blob of paint and mixing it thoroughly with a wet brush or palette knife. A little water added in the same way further dilutes the paint, When mixing more than one color with medium, the separate blobs of color should be mixed together on the palette and the medium then worked in. The paint is brushed thinly on the canvas so the ground shows through, and successive layers can be applied as each dries. A very watered color may need a little gloss or matt medium added to maintain the paint's adhesive properties.

Flat color
Few acrylic colors can be laid as flat color without dilution, and these few need several solid coats of paint applied with a brush or palette knife. Rowney's Flow Formula range, for example, flows and brushes out more easily for painting large areas in opaque color. Well-diluted Flow Formula applied to an unprimed canvas leaves the weave visible as part of the finished painting. Hyplar is a similar range of acrylic colors manufactured by Grumbacher.

Brushing
Brushmarks can be eliminated by brushing a thin layer of diluted paint well into the canvas and then into the weave with a dry rag. After a few minutes a second coat is applied which can be either lighter or darker. When dry, a third coat is applied evenly.

Many styles and techniques can be achieved with acrylic paints and brushmarks can be made into a feature of the work. The British artist Tom Phillips, for example, uses stippling, hatching and dry brushing to achieve particular effects and hard straight edges with masking tape. His acrylic painting *Benches*, which reproduces postcard images, measures 9 feet by 4 feet (2.74m by 1.22m) and consists of three separate canvases. He applied all the paint—19 Aqua-Tec colors—with long, square signwriting brushes.

The dry brushing techniques, used in oil and watercolor painting, can be used with undiluted or diluted acrylic paint. The brush is kept dry, the bristles being fanned under slight pressure during the painting.

Hard edge design and drawing with line
The lines are drawn in pencil for a hard edge design and masking tape is then stuck along the edges. The paint is taken up to and over the tape which is then carefully peeled away. The paint dries and the tape is then stuck on another pencil line. Very fine lines can be drawn by using masking tape according to a finely drawn design—and this is known as drawing with line. Thinned paint is applied with soft sable brushes.

Impastos
The British artist John Bratby (born 1928) makes impastos by squeezing acrylic paint directly on to the canvas. Although this method involves a longer drying time than mixing first on the palette with a little water

or medium and applying with a brush or knife, it adheres to the support immediately. Impastos are made more quickly and easily with acrylic paints than with oils. A textured paste made for impastos can be applied to the support and painted over, but it does not handle like paint and does not reflect the characteristics of an artist's style.

Airbrushing
Acrylic paint can be used in airbrushes in the same way as oils, gouache and watercolors. As with oils, acrylics can be airbrushed on to canvas, board and metal sheets, and walls provided that the surface has been prepared. The smallest form of airbrush today is an atomizer. Airbrushes are precision instruments which can produce extremely fine lines and tonal gradations which give a photographic effect. Those used for delicate work have a small paint or dye reservoir which is filled with an eye-dropper or paint brush. Those used for larger works have a bigger nozzle and a paint reservoir into which the paint is poured. Sprayguns are used for really large areas: the paint is diluted until it is as thin as milk.

Air is blown through the airbrush before filling the reservoir to clear any moisture or dust. It is held like a pen at different angles to the paper, depending on the effect sought. The brush is controlled by pressing the button down for the air supply and backwards for the paint supply. The color can be changed by pouring the paint out of the reservoir, filling it with water and spraying it through until it sprays clear; the reservoir can then be refilled.

Fine lines are drawn by holding the airbrush close to the paper and pressing the control button back very slightly. Straight lines can be drawn by resting the nozzle on the raised edge of a ruler which is held with the other hand, and sliding the nozzle along the ruler while spraying. Colors which contain finely ground pigment are best for fine work.

Flat, evenly colored patches are obtained by spraying opaque paint in parallel lines about 4 inches (10cm) above the paper, each stroke slightly overlapping the last.

Areas of graded tone are achieved by working from the lightest tone to the darkest, again in parallel lines, using a little backward pressure for the first stroke and increasing it with each stroke. A gradation can also be obtained by using a light tone of the color first, mixed on the palette with white, and then a darker tone. Transparent colors are the most suitable for graduating and merging different colors; two colors can be combined to produce a third by this method.

Spattered or mottled effects can be achieved either by fitting a special spatter cap instead of the air cap or by lowering the air pressure, or by pressing the control button back, but not down.

Masks are essential to prevent other parts of the painting being sprayed, and they can be used to define specific shapes and edges. A design can be traced and lightly cut with a scalpel from masking film, a transparent adhesive plastic. The cut pieces of the film are lifted out for airbrushing color on to the painting and are then replaced to protect that piece while another segment is lifted out. A soft or hard edge design can be made using a thin piece of card from which a shape has been cut. The card edge is held a little above the painting and moved after each spraying. The closer the card, the sharper the edge.

Masking fluid can be painted on to form a thin coat of latex over the areas not to be sprayed. Intricate patterns of fine lines and dots can be scored through the latex so that the paint penetrates them—this is a form of hatching and stippling. When the paint is dry the mask is rubbed gently with an eraser and then peeled off.

Other forms of masks include stencils which are available in many shapes and patterns, and pieces of absorbent cotton or cloth.

Cleaning and varnishing

An acrylic painting is waterproof and can be cleaned with soap and water and finally sponged with clean water. Although varnishing is not needed, a matt acrylic varnish can be applied to exterior murals if desired. The varnish can be removed with turpentine or white spirit.

Laying flat, opaque color 1. Apply a broad area of thick paint, using a soft brush.

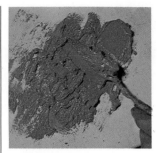

Applying impasto 1. Use the paint thickly, direct from the tube or with added gel. Spread it on the canvas with a knife.

2. Rub over the paint with a clean, dry rag, working the color into the surface and removing the brushmarks.

2. Apply thick blobs of paint with a brush. The adhesive and quick-drying properties of acrylic mean it can be used thickly.

Glazing 1. Mix a small amount of color with a lot of gel or medium. Acrylic mediums are white when wet and reduce the color value.

3. A more transparent glaze can be achieved by adding extra medium. Note that at this stage the color is even further devalued.

3. The paint is used without medium so that it is opaque. Repeat the application if a thick coat of flat color is required.

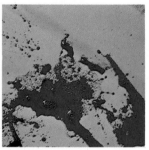

Splattering 1. Mix up thin paint in a small jar. Hold the jar over the canvas and drag paint over the lip of the jar with a brush.

2. Apply the paint with a soft brush. Because acrylic dries so quickly, it can be supplied in any thickness, layer by layer.

4. Glazes may be laid in smooth layers over a stained or painted area, but can also be applied thickly, showing brushmarks.

Laying broken color Load a brush with undiluted paint. Draw the brush lightly across the surface of the canvas.

2. The splattering makes an irregular pattern. Allow it to dry and repeat with another color, or use a glaze or stain over the top.

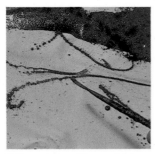

3. Fine splattered lines and drips are made by flicking a brush loaded with wet paint over the canvas.

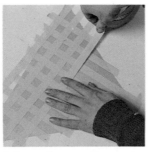

4. Lay another area of tape, and paint over the whole with diluted medium. Let it dry.

2. Hold the mask firmly on the canvas and paint over the shape. Work away from the cut edges. The paint must not be too wet.

Collage with paint. Collage can also be done using acrylic paint which has adhesive properties.

Masking with tape 1. Lay tape firmly along the edges of the required shape. Paint over the whole area with diluted medium.

5. Paint over the taped area with a different color, taking care not to disturb the edges of the tape. The paint must not be too wet.

3. Lift the piece of card away from the canvas to check that the painted area is clean and sharp. Remove the piece of card.

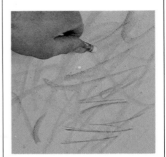

Acrylic paint over oil crayon 1. Draw on the canvas with oil crayons. Build up the crayoned marks quite thickly.

2. Paint evenly over the whole shape, working over and away from the edges of the tape towards the center.

6. Peel back the tape carefully. Any number of layers can be built up, but each must be dry before more tape is used.

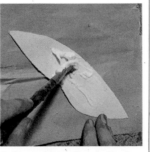

Collage with medium 1. Acrylic medium can be used for collaging. Cut a canvas shape and paint one side with medium.

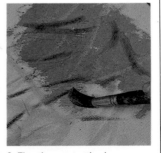

2. Thin the paint with a large amount of water and brush it lightly over the crayoned area with a large soft brush.

3. Let the painted shape dry thoroughly. Lift one corner of the tape and peel it back carefully from the canvas.

Masking with card 1. Draw the required shape on a thin piece of card and cut it out with a knife. Use masking film or tape.

2. Press the shape, glue side downwards, on to a stretched canvas. Rub over the back with a clean, dry brush.

3. The oil crayon resists the paint and the drawing shows up clearly through the colored wash.

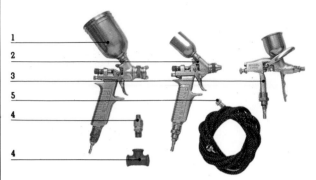

Sprayguns Sprayguns used with acrylic paint have larger nozzles and reservoirs than normal airbrushes. The range includes the DeVilbiss MPS (**1**), DeVilbiss MP (**2**), and Binks Bullows L90 (**3**). Also important are adaptors (**4**) and the hose (**5**).

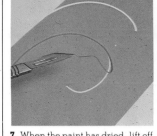

7. When the paint has dried, lift off the tape carefully, using a scalpel if necessary, to reveal the pattern.

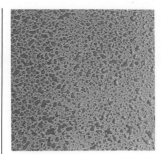

Blotting 1. Another effect can be achieved by spraying water on to the surface and, before it dries, spraying on paint.

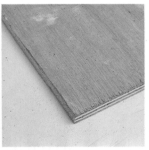

Masking 1. Different types of masks — such as wood, paper or tape — can be used to achieve a variety of effects.

4. Using a tape and paper mask gives the sharpest line of all.

8. Masking fluid can be sprayed through the gun to create a pattern.

2. When the paint has dried but the water is still wet, blot the water off with absorbent paper or a sponge.

2. A wood mask gives a soft edge. Do not stick the wood down, just place it on the surface.

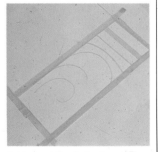

5. Mask out the desired area. The masking tape can be curved and used to create positive or negative lines.

9. On top of the dried masking fluid, spray a layer of paint.

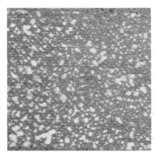

3. The paper lifts off the water and leaves a mottled effect where the paint has dried and the water has not.

3. A paper mask produces a much sharper line because it is thinner than the wood. Again, do not stick the paper down.

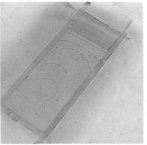

6. Spray and even area of color over the masked area. Work horizontally and vertically with even strokes.

10. When the paint has dried, rub off the masking fluid with your hand. This leaves a distinctive mottled pattern.

Different pressures Spraying with varying pressures creates different effects from an even spread of color to a clear dot pattern.

Watercolor.

History. Supports. Stretching paper. Equipment: Paints, Brushes, Easels, Water. **Techniques:** Alla prima, Washes, Stippling, Scumbling, Dry brush technique.

Watercolor History

ransparency and the soft harmony of color washes, with highlights and lighter areas rendered by leaving the white paper bare or faintly toned, are the main characteristics of 'pure' watercolor painting.

The color cannot be worked on its ground to the same extent as with oils or other opaque media—errors cannot be merely painted over, for instance—so that a higher initial standard of technique may be involved to produce a satisfactory watercolor painting. But the freshness and brilliance of a good watercolor are ample compensation for the time spent in acquiring sound technique.

Since the time of the ancient Egyptians, water has been used as a diluent in many types of paint, including size paint, distemper, fresco, tempera and gouache. True watercolor, however, consists solely of very finely ground pigment with gum arabic (known sometimes as gum senegal) as the binder.

The water-soluble gum acts as a light varnish, giving the colors a greater brightness and sheen.

Other substances may occasionally be added to the water in making up the actual paint, including sugar syrup and glycerin. The syrup acts as a plasticizer, making the painting smoother; and the glycerin is said to lend extra brilliance and in warm weather prevents the paint from drying too quickly.

White pigment is never used in a pure watercolor palette. Its addition creates, in effect, a different medium—gouache.

Although many medieval illustrators used pure—that is transparent—watercolor in small works and on manuscripts, others added opaque or body color to make a background on which gold leaf was laid. The first European fully to recognize the value of the medium in larger works, using it extensively in landscape paintings, was the German artist Albrecht Dürer (1471–1528). Although strong lines and opaque passages played their part, the unique transparency of watercolor washes was a major feature of these works.

One of the earliest English artists to make full and effective use of the medium was John White, a draftsman with Sir Walter Raleigh's 1585 expedition to the coast of North America. White's use of the full range of watercolor in clean washes when making drawings for the record of the life and scenery of the North Carolina coast have caused some historians to claim him as the 'father' of the English watercolor school.

Indeed, on the Continent, watercolor became known as 'the English art'; but it was not until nearly two centuries later, in the latter part of the eighteenth century, that the art blossomed into its full pride and distinction in the hands of such painters as Paul Sandby (1725–1809), William Blake (1757–1827), Thomas Girtin (1755–1802), J.M.W. Turner (1755–1851), John Crome (1763–1821), John Sell Cotman (1782–1842), John

Varley (1778–1842), David Cox (1783–1859), and Peter de Wint (1784–1849).

Only those who have mastered a basic technique and recognized the limitations of a medium can afford to depart from the rules and, in doing so, evolve new styles. Thomas Girtin, for instance, regarded the limitations of watercolor as a challenge and, in effect, increased the challenge by deliberately restricting the range of his palette. He used only five basic colors: yellow ochre, burnt sienna, light red, monastral blue and ivory black. He applied the paint in thin washes, allowing each wash to dry before applying the next, building up deep tonal gradations and contrasts. Like most of the 'English school' he left areas of white paper untouched to provide highlights; but occasionally, and effectively, broke a 'rule' by using gouache for the odd highlight.

William Blake devised something akin to offset printing to apply his first layers of color, painting on an impervious surface such as glass, porcelain or a glazed card or paper, and pressing this over his painting paper. When the 'print' was dry, he worked over it in opaque or body color to elaborate and enliven it.

J.M.W. Turner virtually forced the paint to obey his rules, shifting it while wet, scumbling and scratching it on heavy paper until gleaming and glowing effects were produced—unrecognizable at first as true watercolor. He mixed techniques and made them compatible. In *Tintern Abbey* he built up strong tonal contrasts with flat and broken washes. Heavy wet-into-wet methods, scumbles and dry-brush strokes were all combined in the harmonies of *Kilgarran Castle*; while *Venice from the Ciudecca* is alive with thin, wet washes and delicate touches of opaque paint.

The Victorian age saw a rise in the general popularity of watercolor painting, particularly in Britain; and some Victorian artists, including John Everett Millais (1829–1896), found a ready sale for watercolor copies of their larger oil paintings. Watercolor had already been used for the opposite process—making quick color sketches for later rendering as larger works in oil—by such masters as van Dyck (1599–1641), Gainsborough (1727–1788) and Constable (1776–1837).

They discovered that quick-drying watercolor enabled them to experiment with color contrasts and make swift notes of passing atmospheric effects, such as mists, rainbows, changing reflections and fast-altering cloud formations.

America's tradition of watercolor painting, although not so long as that of England, is soundly based on the work of fine exponents like Winslow Homer (1830–1910) who did much for the art in the States (although appreciation was slow to come: fine paintings of his were selling for as little as 75 dollars in 1880). The tradition was carried on by Thomas Eakins (1844–1916), Edward Hopper (1882–1967) and Andrew Wyeth (born 1917). Ben Shahn (1898–1969) used the medium with great fluidity especially in the expression of social ideas, exemplified by his *Martin Luther King* painted in 1966.

The English tradition has been carried on strongly by such major artists as Edward Burra (1905–1976), Paul Nash (1889–1946) and David Jones (born 1895). In Europe, Paul Klee (1879–1940), a founder member of the Bauhaus, used watercolor for some of his most significant work. His *Motif of Mammamet* shows a striking use of colors contrasted in small, rough-edged, carefully-proportioned washes which reveal the texture of the paper beneath.

The distinction between fine art and the art of the illustrator, always blurred, became more so in the nineteenth century with the invention of half-tone

reproduction. Overlaying of red, yellow and blue inks, broken down by screens to produce many tones, made possible the reproduction of illustrations in full color. Watercolor was found to be an ideal medium to submit to the process, which enabled books containing full-color illustrations to be produced comparatively cheaply for the mass market. Among the many fine artists who used watercolor for their illustration originals are Rackham (1867–1939) and Edmund Dulac (1882–1953). Dulac outlined and pointed up many of his drawings with Indian ink. In printing—although the black itself could not be reproduced by the three-color process—this tended to soften and enhance the watercolor washes lying within his outlines.

Watercolor Supports

The most widely-used watercolor support is paper, which is manufactured for the purpose in a wide variety of weights and textures.

Ignoring the many cheap papers made up into children's 'drawing and painting books', there are three main categories of real watercolor paper: hot-pressed or HP; cold-pressed (CP)—also known as 'not' paper in Britain ('not' for 'not hot-pressed'); and rough.

Hot-pressed is very smooth, and suitable for line and wash. Many artists find it too slippery for pure watercolor work. Cold-pressed is the most popular all-round paper. Its semi-rough surface takes large, even washes very well, but a quickly-dragged dryish brush will also bring up what roughness it possesses, so that smooth and rough surfaces are obtainable on the same sheet. Fine detail can also be rendered on cold-pressed paper.

Rough paper has a definite 'tooth' to it. It drags at the brush. This produces a speckled effect, with pigment settling in the lower parts of the surface, leaving the rest white. This is fine for rendering, say, the sparkle of sunshine on water; but the overall appearance of the picture is inclined to be monotonous in the hands of a beginner if he or she cannot achieve, as contrast, the deep, even, wet washes which the expert can produce on the roughest paper.

Hand-made papers are of the highest quality—and the most expensive. They are mainly of pure linen rag, bleached without chemicals, or with chemicals which are thoroughly neutralized; and they are sized on one side only. This correct painting side faces the artist when the paper, held up to the light, shows the maker's water-mark the right way round.

Japanese rice papers, fragile and absorbent, are

obtainable in Europe and America; and some Western artists have experimented with them successfully for delicate work. Those available include Kozo, Mitsumata and Gambi. Kozo is the strongest.

Tinted papers are sometimes used, especially for reproduction work; but the basic tint may not be as permanent as the colors laid on it, and its change could affect the overall tone of the picture in time. Many artists prefer to apply their own tint with a very thin wash and a sponge.

The weight or thickness of a watercolor paper is as important a consideration as its surface. Weight is measured by the ream. A 70lb paper, for instance, means that 480 sheets of it—a ream—weighs 70lb.

Light papers may need stretching to prevent them buckling under heavy washes. Heavier papers, of 140lb and upwards, can be clipped to a board and used for direct work.

In general, the weight of the paper, and its price, increases in proportion to the size of the ready-cut sheets, so that an artist who wishes to use a heavier paper in a smaller size may have to cut it from a larger sheet. However, the medium and most popular size, 30 by 22in (75 by 55cm) has the greatest range of weights associated with it: from 70lb to 300lb.

Names associated with good artists' papers include Saunders, R.W.S. (Royal Watercolour Society), Bockingford, Crisbrook, d'Arches, Arnold, Green, Fabriano, Michallet and Ingres. Hand-made papers include the 90lb R.W.S., Saunders, and tinted Fabriano paper.

A good paper for beginners in the medium is Saunders machine-made 90lb, 30 by 22in, with cold-pressed surface. It is tough, stretches well if needed to take heavy washes and stands up well to drawing and erasing.

A wide range of papers similar to the best made in Britain, France and Italy is manufactured in America by the Strathmore Paper Company.

All watercolor papers should be stored in as dry a place as possible. Damp may activate chemical impurities producing spots which will not take color.

Watercolor paper Good handmade or machine made papers for watercolor painting will have a clearly visible watermark (**left**). The right side of the paper to work on is the side on which the watermark can be seen the right way round. Three main surfaces (**below**) are available (from **left** to **right**) hot-pressed, a fairly smooth surface, not (or cold pressed) paper, which is semi-rough, and rough.

Types of watercolor paper A number of manufacturers produce excellent papers for watercolor work. A number of different examples are shown **below.** When a paper is selected the weight, texture and tone required must be carefully considered. It may be preferable to use white paper and, if a tint is required, apply a wash of paint all over to achieve the right color, but a good range of tinted papers is available. The texture should be chosen according to how much white will be seen through the paint. A smooth paper will rapidly become covered with color, but the heavily textured papers leave tiny white flecks showing through a watercolor wash.

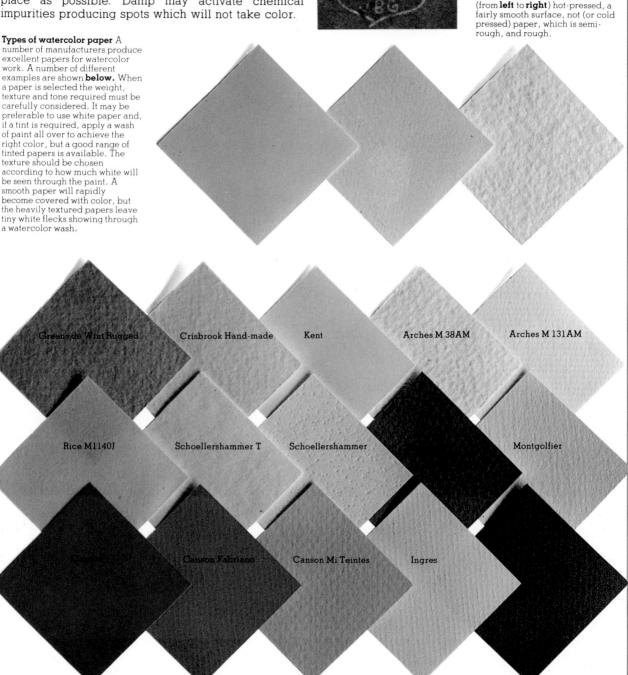

Greens de Wint Rugged

Crisbrook Hand-made

Kent

Arches M 38AM

Arches M 131AM

Rice M1140J

Schoellershammer T

Schoellershammer

Montgolfier

Canson Fabriano

Canson Mi Teintes

Ingres

Watercolor Stretching Paper

ighter-weight papers, which tend to buckle when washes are applied, should be stretched before use. There are a number of different methods.

The simplest, for studio use, is to wet the paper thoroughly by laying it in a tray of water. Holding it by the edge, shake off the surplus water and lay the paper, painting surface up, on a drawing board, preferably of a size which gives 2in (5cm) clearance all round from the margin of the paper. Stick the edges down with strips from a roll of gummed brown paper. Put a drawing pin (thumbtack) in each corner. As the painting paper dries, it will pull itself smooth and tight.

For field work, some artists use a light panel of wood or Masonite smaller than the cut paper. Two or three sheets of dampened paper are laid over the thin board, folded down and under, and held in place with a number of spring clips. The toughness of the dried stretched paper holds it in place when the clips are removed; and a completed sheet can be taken off without disturbing the lower sheets.

Ready-prepared watercolor boards—light papers mounted on cardboard—are pleasant to use and do not of course need stretching. But they are more expensive than paper and heavy to carry in quantity.

Home-made boards, with light paper strongly glued to pasteboard, can be satisfactory for practice; but paper should always be glued to the back of these boards to prevent buckling.

Special stretching-frames or striators can be bought, on to which heavier weights of paper can be stretched and held taut, with the edges crimped between an inner and an outer framework. These are for experts, providing a pleasant 'give' to the paper similar to that of an oil canvas. But even experts have been known to hole their wash-weakened paper; and some artists believe that such stretching adversely affects the surface texture of the paper.

Paper samples Manufacturers often produce small swatches of paper samples, which enable the artist to compare the different weights and textures of the various types. As the quality papers are quite expensive, there may be a charge for a sample swatch, but it is very useful reference material for artists working mainly in watercolor.

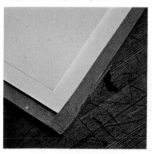

Stretching paper 1. Check which is the right side of the paper. Hold it to the light so the watermark appears the right way round.

3. Soak the paper in a tray or sink full of clean water. The amount of time needed to soak varies with the type of paper.

5. Take the paper out of water and drain it off. Lay it on the board and stick dampened gummed tape along one side.

2. Trim the paper to size for the drawing board, leaving a good margin of board so that the gummed tape will adhere.

4. Measure out lengths of gummed paper tape to match each side of the drawing board.

6. Stick gum strip along the opposite side of the paper. Tape the other two sides. Keep the paper quite flat throughout.

7. To secure the paper, push a drawing pin into the board at each corner. Let the paper dry naturally or it may split.

51

Watercolor Equipment

Paints

In buying watercolors, price more accurately reflects the quality than in any other medium. Large, cheap multi-hued boxes of so-called watercolor, muddy, impermanent, and consisting more of filler than pigment, may delight the eye of a child but are useless for serious work. 'Students' Colors', usually put in smaller boxes or in tube-color sets, are good for practice especially if made by a reputable firm. But only those paints labelled 'Artists' Colors' can be relied upon to give the transparency, glow and permanency that the keen artist, professional or amateur, requires.

In this expensive, highest-quality range, there is no essential difference—except in terms of portability and convenience—between 'solid' and tube colors. The quality names to keep in mind are Winsor and Newton, Rowney, Reeves and Grumbacher.

Dry cakes and semi-moist pans are little-used nowadays; half-pans, also semi-moist, are the best-known form. The best-quality half-pans can be bought singly in their tiny white boxes, and are often sold as sets in small flattish tins which double as palettes.

Semi-liquid tubes of watercolor are preferred by artists who wish to apply large washes. Fully liquid watercolor can be bought in bottles, with an eyedropper provided to transfer paint to palette. Good ranges include Luma and Dr. Martin's. It is obviously quicker to use these, or the watered-down 'liquid' tube color, then to lift color from a half-pan with a wet brush to make up a wash.

Few watercolor artists, even the most expert, would claim to use more than 11 or 12 colors, from which the whole range could be mixed. But early English watercolorists, like Thomas Girtin, painted masterpieces using a palette of no more than five basic, permanent colors. There is certainly no need for any artist to keep any more than 10 or 11 colors.

An adequate modern palette is: ivory black, Payne's gray (optional), burnt umber, cadmium red, yellow ochre, cadmium yellow, Hooker's green, viridian, monastral blue, French ultramarine and Alizarin crimson.

Professional artists may argue about the 'best' basic palette, but few would disagree that a beginner or early student is best advised to stick to a restricted palette, which not only forces him or her to consider the basics of color mixing but imposes a pleasing harmony and consistency on the finished work.

Some pigments with a chemical dye base will stain paper rather than create a transparent wash on the surface. The 'stainers', which might be quite useful for certain purposes, can be quite easily discovered: blob the color on paper and let it dry. Then rinse under running water. 'Stain' pigments will remain.

Purists—and experimenters—can make their own watercolors at home or in the studio—a time-consuming process, but some may find it worthwhile. They will need finely-ground pigments of the finest quality, a plate glass slab, a grinding miller or muller, a plastic palette knife or spatula, and gum arabic, glycerin, distilled water, ox gall, sugar solution and carbolic acid solution.

Pour one part of mixed sugar and glycerin solution plus two or three parts of gum arabic and a few drops of ox gall into a little pool on the glass. Then, with the palette knife, slowly draw in and mix the little heap of pigment placed beside it until there is a stiff paste. Grind this with the muller, and scrape the mixture into a pan.

Brushes

The patient craft of the brushmaker is tested to the full in making brushes that meet the demands of watercolor artists. They want flat or chisel brushes that lay good even washes, and brushes that can be drawn to a fine point to render detail as well as lay a lot of color in one even stroke.

In the various sizes that are also demanded, the nearest to a perfect bristle that the brushmakers have found is red sable, from the tail hairs of Siberian mink. These make the most expensive but the longest-lasting of brushes, providing they are well cared-for.

Squirrel (so-called 'camel') hair, and ox hair are the best substitutes. Man-made fibers—synthetics—have still to make an adequate mark as far as artists are concerned.

The very fine brushes (000, 00 and 0) are rarely used. Fine is reckoned to start with 1, going through to 12. A beginner's range might well start with 4, 8 and 12 in the 'rounds', plus a ½in or 1in (1.25 or 2.5cm) flat. The choice is personal, depending on what the artist needs to do.

Chinese hogshair brushes are now available in the West: long-handled (bamboo), with the bristles tightly-bunched for delicate, fine-point work.

Easels

There are many types of easels, most of which can be set and adjusted for watercolor work. The delicate—it might almost be described as intimate—work of watercolor is best carried out at close quarters, either with the board-mounted surface propped up on a table in the studio, or rested on the knees or a light, specialized easel in the field.

Watercolor easels range from the neck strap and board for sketching to well-patented collapsible wood and aluminium contraptions, to the satchel for materials which converts to an outdoors stool.

Water

In materials, consider the most important adjunct of all: the water. Use distilled water whenever possible. Over-hard or too soft water can play strange tricks with paper and colors. Carry the water in a large screw-top bottle if painting outdoors; and tip it into two jars—one for washing the brushes, one for slaking the colors: delicate tints can easily be muddied by using water in which brushes have been washed.

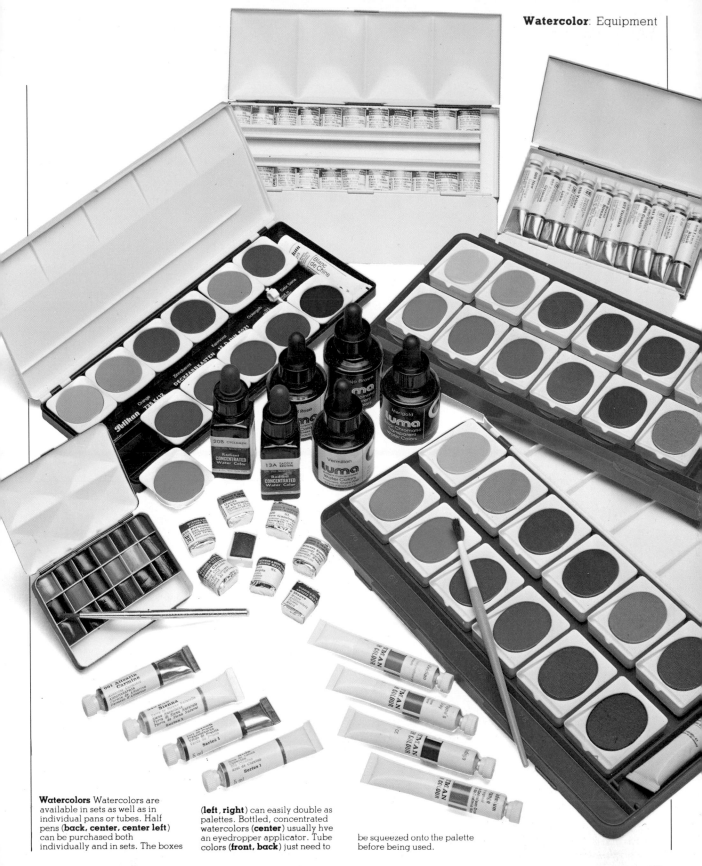

Watercolors Watercolors are available in sets as well as in individual pans or tubes. Half pens (**back, center, center left**) can be purchased both individually and in sets. The boxes (**left, right**) can easily double as palettes. Bottled, concentrated watercolors (**center**) usually hve an eyedropper applicator. Tube colors (**front, back**) just need to be squeezed onto the palette before being used.

53

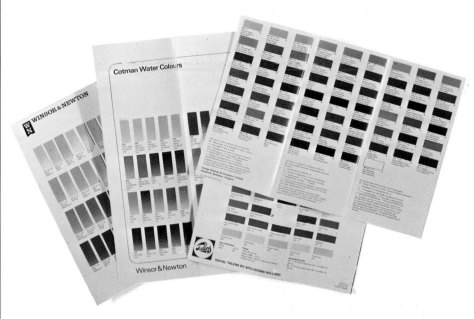

Watercolors and brushes A wide range of watercolors is available, and the manufacturers produce charge of all the colors available in each range (**left**). It is common to find that a single manufacturer may produce more than one range, one of which will be more expensive and better quality than any others. The lower quality ranges are produced by avoiding the use of expensive pigments, and usually an attempt is made to standardize prices. There will be differences also between the flow and permanence of the different quality paints. Soft sable brushes are best for most techniques, and these are produced in different series by several manufacturers. This selection of size five brushes from different series (**below**) indicates the variations. The brushes are (from **left** to **right**): Proarte Series 1 and 3, LP Series 38, Winsor and Newton Series 7, LP Series 1A, Winsor and Newton Series 3A, 16, and 33. The Winsor and Newton Series 7 is the highest quality red sable brush available.

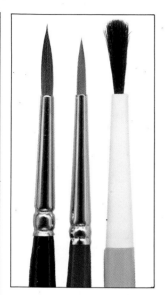

Types of brushes Many watercolor boxes include a brush, but these are often of very poor quality, as can be seen (**left**) in a comparison (from **left** to **right**) between a best quality sable brush, a synthetic sable and the extremely cheap type of brush sometimes found in boxes. The series of brushes (**right**) shows all the different sizes available in one type of brush. Japanese bamboo brushes (**right below**) are versatile and convenient both for covering large areas and for detailed work with the brush tip. A range of brushes suitable for watercolor painting are shown **below** (from **left** to **right**): blender, fine synthetic roundhair, broad synthetic round hair, mixed fibers round, ox hair round, squirrel hair round, sable fan bright, sable round, fine sable round.

Japanese inks and brushes
Watercolor painting techniques are traditionally associated with ink drawing and wash. To some extent, painting with stick inks combines the two types of work. Soft brushes are used, set in bamboo handles, which can be splayed out for broad sweeps of color, or drawn up to a very fine point for line work. This small ink set (**left**), produced by Grumbacher, gives one colored ink and black, and a fine bamboo brush. Several sizes of brush are available. The materials may be used in the manner of ink or watercolor, or combined with ordinary water-based paints.

Rags and sponges As the characteristic feature of watercolor painting is the extreme liquidity of the paint, rags and sponges (**below**) are very useful both as painting utensils and to control or mop up the paint if it runs too much. Paint dabbed on with a sponge has a rich, rough texture.

Principles of watercolor painting The essential feature of watercolor painting, which makes it different from other techniques, is that the color values are reduced only by the addition of water, never by adding white paint, and the paint is thus always transparent. These two examples of different dilutions of watercolor paint (**right**) serve to illustrate this point. A strong hue may be applied to the paper by adding only enough water to the paint to make it flow evenly. The traditional watercolor technique, however, is to allow the strength of the color to build up in the painting by successive applications of thin washes of dilute, transparent color, leaving bare patches of paper for white highlights. The brilliance of the white paper also emerges through the thin paint layers, which gives watercolors their clarity and luminosity.

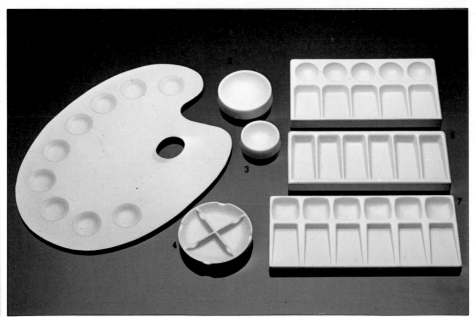

Palettes Recessed or well palettes must be used for mixing watercolor, so that any quantity of water required can be added and colors cannot flow together. Palettes of ceramic material, plastic or metal are suitable, and are available in a variety of different sizes and shapes. It is really a matter of personal choice whether a separate small pot (**2**, **3**) is used for each color, or whether the paints are kept together in a large palette with several wells (**4**, **5**, **6**, **7**). The traditional kidney shaped palette with a thumb hole (**1**), which can be held in the hand while painting, may be more useful for outdoor work where flat surfaces may not be available, but for studio work no one style is more valuable than another. If extra palette room is needed, ordinary plates and saucers are quite suitable and the paint is easily washed away afterwards.

Easels for watercolor Before buying an easel the watercolorist should give careful consideration to his or her requirements. A large variety of easels is now available, so the artist should be able to find a suitable one without difficulty. The best studio easels can be adjusted to a horizontal position for sketching. Many watercolorists work outside. For this type of painting, some artists prefer to work with only a drawing board and pad, but there are many collapsible lightweight easels that are also suitable. Some portable easels are provided with a compartment for carrying materials. Generally, aluminium easels are cheaper than wooden ones. However, as these easels are very light, it is advisable to buy one that has spikes on the feet to hold the easel firm in windy conditions or on soft ground. The

sketching easel (**1**) has rubber tipped feet but it can be supplied with spikes if required. It is made from beechwood, a very hard-wearing wood. The adjustable legs enable the artist to work at a comfortable height. When fully extended this easel will hold a canvas at a fixed height, either in a vertical position or tilted forward to any desired angle. It is easy to carry, weighing only 3¾lbs (1.6 kg). The aluminium sketching easel (**2**) is slightly larger. It is fully adjustable. A disadvantage of this easel is that it only has rubber feet which will not always keep the easel steady. The aluminium table easel (**3**) is extremely light. When not in use it folds up very compactly and can be stored out of the way. The radial studio easel (**4**) is made of wood and it can also be folded to take up less space. The easel may

be tilted backwards and forwards as well as the canvas which can be moved to a horizontal position. There is an extra large wing nut to lock the easel steady. The combination easel (**5**), made of seasoned beechwood, is both a folding studio easel and a drawing table. This makes it extremely practical for artists who have small studios. It will take a very wide canvas, tilted at any angle or kept in an upright position. When it is used as a drawing table, the frame for the drawing board can be adjusted easily to a comfortable height. The frame will hold drawing boards of any standard size or type. A useful piece of equipment for artists who work outdoors is the combined satchel and stool (**6**). A strap is attached to the light metal legs of the stool so it is easy to carry. All the artist's materials, such as paints, brushes

1

2

3

4

and paper can be put in the satchel. Another easel for outdoor work is the combined sketching seat and easel (**7**). This versatile easel can be used with canvas, block, frame and sketching board. It is fully adjustable to any position. When folded up, it is easily carried by the handle attached to the seat.

Drawing board with strap If the artist is sketching a moving subject, a drawing board with a strap attached may well prove useful. The strap is passed around the artist's neck leaving the hands free for work and allowing him or her to walk around.

5

6

7

Watercolor Techniques

Alla prima Getting the effect right first time around—or *alla prima*—is one of the most difficult watercolor techniques. This accepted representational technique relies on two steps: laying down a thin accurate pencil drawing and filling in with wash, leaving bare paper to provide highlights.

The watercolor painter must work dark on light—never light on dark, as is possible with the oil painter. And strictly speaking, the number of wash overlays should be no more than three, or the overall effect will be muddy. Depth of tone can be lightened after the picture is finished by mopping water over the area with a sponge, blotting paper or absorbent tissues. If the painting is quite dry, tones can be lightened by cross-hatching, or even one-way scraping, with a sharp blade. Purists may wince, but it is most important for the final result to satisfy the artist.

Washes The chief characteristic of all watercolor painting is the wash—flat, variegated in the same tone, or subtly changing from one tone to another.

To lay a flat wash, dampen the whole area to be painted, use a large flat brush and make up sufficient color—which is usually more than you think will be needed. Do this quickly so that the brush strokes flow into each other.

Practice with the board tilted so that the strokes flow downwards into each other, but do not paint downwards—all the strokes should be horizontal. Mop at the bottom of the wash with a dry brush, rag or tissue. Dampen a complicated edge or outline around which the wash is laid, to keep the color from straying.

A gradated wash is laid by progressively strengthening color in the palette as the strokes are made. It is best to lay the dark edge first, and keep in mind that color becomes lighter as it dries.

For variegated washes, mix the colors first. Use no more than three. Let each color dry before using the next, then, when all are dry, sponge or brush them together. In this way, the directness and delicacy of the colors are preserved.

Stippling Stippling is a method of applying color in dots which are mixed by the eye into a tone. Georges Seurat, of the Impressionist school, used it most effectively. It can be employed as a contrast to wash, or over a wash. Use a fine brush, working from the outside of the area to be covered in towards the center.

Scumbling Scumbling means applying the paint with a scrubbing motion so that it is worked into the paper from all directions. It picks up the texture of the surface in a most effective way, but it should not be overused or it can lead to a monotonous overall effect.

Dry brush technique This uses the minimum of color on a fine point to apply the color and is most effective in rendering detail. But dry brush can also be employed, especially in landscape work, to produce broad effects. Spread the bristles below the ferrule with thumb and forefinger. The paint emerges as fine separated lines of color.

Other techniques Pen line and watercolor wash are often used together for their own special and sometimes startling effect, with line defining the drawing and wash blocking-in the outlines. But it is possible, and often effective, to lay the washes first then point up, outline and shade with line. Only practice can decide for the artist which method suits him or her.

Sponges are used by many artists not only to apply broad washes, giving their own special effect, but to lighten tones. A perfectly clean sponge must be used for the latter purpose. Wet the paint then gently 'massage' it with the half-dry sponge. Leave for a few minutes, then mop up the excess water with blotting paper. Repeat the process if necessary until the right tone is achieved.

An eraser can be used to reduce the intensity of a wash. But the paint must be completely dry and the eraser quite clean. The texture of the paper can be picked up by this method and—as J.M.W. Turner discovered—erasure itself can be used as a painting technique.

An even splatter of paint droplets can be achieved with a clean toothbrush. Load the brush with fairly stiff paint, hold it above the paper, and draw a stiff knife across the bristles. By masking areas of the paper, whole pictures can be 'painted' by this method.

Both gum arabic and soap can be added to paint to make 'scratching back' easier. Soap makes it possible to paint on surfaces that would otherwise reject watercolor, such as glass or plastics. Another use for it is to make initial imprints of natural objects like flowers, grasses, leaves and feathers. Coat one side of the objects with soap, apply paint over the soap, then press the object on to paper. The method is sometimes so effective that the imprint does not need retouching.

Masking fluid is sometimes used to leave untouched areas of paper, enabling a wash to be quickly applied. It can be peeled off after the wash has been laid. Candle wax is occasionally used for the same 'resist' purpose, but this cannot be removed and must be left as an integral part of the painting.

Watercolor techniques include air-brushing, which can apply the color from a thin pencil line to a broad spray. This is mainly used in commercial work, employing very finely-ground paint usually on a hot-pressed surface.

Watercolor techniques

The two crucial elements in watercolor painting are the paper and the paint. In this type of painting, the paper is not just used as a surface to which the paint is applied; the paper also influences the color of the paint, which is transparent. The whiteness of the paper can be used as the white in the painting, and for lightening the tones of paint in the picture. The fundamental watercolor technique is the wash. A wash is a thin layer of translucent color which is applied to the stretched paper. When dry, a wash can be overlaid with another layer, and this darkens the tones. There are several main types of wash. The basic flat wash involves laying flat color over an area too large to be covered by a single brushstroke. A gradated wash is in many ways a technique similar to the flat wash except the color is gradually made darker by using various tones of the same color. A variegated wash combines different colors so that they flow together. It is important in watercolor work that the washes should not be heavy or labored. A watercolor painting should be characterized by an impression of lightness.

In watercolor work there is an extremely close link between the painting technique and the palette of colors which the artist chooses. The artist's palette for watercolor painting does not need to be large; indeed, restricting yourself to a limited number of colors can have positive advantages. A range of about half a dozen colors is ample for the beginner and a dozen is about as many as the experienced watercolor artist would normally need. With this type of painting, it is especially important for the artist to experiment and practice and to get to know his or her palette thoroughly. If you find you need a new color, try mixing colors rather than selecting a completely new one. One major advantage of using a restricted palette is that it will give the painting an overall unity of color tone. A small palette can also be used with ease out of door doors. The British eighteenth century watercolor artist, Thomas Girtin, often used a palette of only five colors — light red, yellow ochre, burnt sienna, monastral blue amd ivory black. By mixing the colors and using dark and light washes, Girtin demonstrated the versatility of the medium. A possible larger palette might include two reds (such as cadmium red and Alizarin red), two yellows (for example yellow ochre and cadmium yellow), two greens (possibly viridian and Hooker's green), and two blues (such as monastral blue and ultramarine).Burnt umber and ivory black complete the range.

Laying a flat wash 1. Tip up the drawing board so that it lies at an angle. Rest one end on a piece of wood to keep it steady.

2. Keep two pots of water to hand, one quite clean for dampening paper. Use broad-based, wide-necked jars such as jam jars.

3. Dampen the paper using a large brush and clean water. Make sure that it is thoroughly damp, but not too wet.

4. Mix color with water in a palette. Mix up enough to cover the whole area to be painted so that it will have an even tone.

5. Lay a broad line of color on the dampened area of the paper, working evenly in one direction only.

6. Lay another line directly under the first, working back in the opposite direction. Allow the color to spread and even out.

7. Continue working from side to side in broad sweeps of color until the whole area is completely covered with paint.

Gradated wash A gradated wash looks very different when it is applied to a rough paper (**left**) and a smooth one (**right**).

Laying a gradated wash 1. Damp the paper as before. Mix up some color and lay a line of paint at full color strength.

2. Dilute the paint and lay in a second line of lighter color, directly under the first. Repeat with successively lighter tones.

Laying a variegated wash 1. Dampen an area of paper for the wash with clean water. It is sometimes convenient to use a sponge.

2. Mix up some paint and lay in the first color over part of the paper, letting it flow from the brush in an irregular shape.

3. Mix and lay in a second color in an irregular shape as before. Let it spread slightly into the first color but not flood it.

Stippling Use a fine brush to make tiny dots of paint. Keep the pressure even. Vary brush size or pressure for a coarser texture.

2. Fan out the bristles of the brush between thumb and finger and draw the brush over the surface of the paper.

3. To obtain a straight line while the wash is still damp, hold a ruler at an angle to the paper and work along it with a brush.

4. Repeat the process with a third color. Any number of colors can be laid in this way. Let the wash dry out before making changes.

Thickening the paint Add gum arabic to the paint to make it thick and glossy. Mix colors on the paper to create a rich texture.

3. For dry brush technique, use either a round hair brush fanned out or a chisel-shaped brush.

Laying a wash against a complicated edge 1. Draw in an outline lightly with pencil. Dampen the paper up to the line.

5. If the color is too strong or too wet, blot gently with blotting paper to control the flow of the paint.

Scumbling Load the brush with paint but keep it fairly dry. Work over the paper with a circular motion.

Wash and line 1. Lay an area of flat wash with a broad brush. Make sure that the wash is not too damp before adding line.

2. Work in color over the damp area of the design, letting the paint spread slowly into the shape of the drawn line.

Splattering Pick up paint on an old toothbrush and hold it over the paper. Run a knife gently up through the bristles of the brush.

Dry brush 1. Load the brush with paint and wipe away surplus moisture on a piece of blotting paper.

2. Use pen and ink to draw in lines over the wash. A crisp line is obtained where the wash is quite dry. In wet areas the line fans out.

3. Once the edge is completed, work away from the line with a broad area of wash until the required amount is covered.